BRING US HOME FROM SORROW

A Love Letter

Joanne Fedler

*For my sisters Carolyn and Laura
and Jess, Aidan and Jenna.
And for every tender heart mourning
the empty place at their table*

Bring Us Home From Sorrow
Copyright©2026 Joanne Fedler
Paperback ISBN: 978-1-76109-723-2
ebook ISBN: 978-1-76109-724-9
First published 2026 by
Ginninderra Press
PO Box 2 Bentleigh 3204
ginninderrapress.com.au

Other Titles by Joanne Fedler

The Whale's Last Song, Harper Collins, 2024
Gagman, with Dov Fedler, Brio books, 2022
Unbecoming, Penguin, 2020
Your Story: how to write it so others will want to read it, Hay House, 2017
Love in the Time of Contempt, Hardie Grant, 2016
Leaning into Love, with Graeme Friedman, Random House, 2012
The Reunion, Allen & Unwin, 2012
When Hungry, Eat, Allen & Unwin, 2010
Things Without a Name, Allen & Unwin, 2008
Secret Mothers' Business, Allen & Unwin, 2006
The Dreamcloth, Jacana Media, 2005

Connect with Joanne here: joannefedler.com
Substack: https://joannefedler.substack.com/
Instagram: @joannefedlermedia.com

Praise for *Bring Us Home From Sorrow*

Joanne doesn't skirt or blink the responsibilities of heartache, but carries her grief as a gift, writing so that the reader will be less lost. This journey through grief is a mothering of culture to help navigate present-day chaos and sorrow. So many love-zingers. This book serves life, now.

—Nathalie Roy, shepherdess, co-founder of Orphan Wisdom School & founder of The Scriptorium, housing Stephen Jenkinson's collected works

Invigorating and thunderous, painful, soothing and nourishing, these pages are as immersive, exacting and jubilant as the author's own experience navigating the riptides and muscularity of the ocean she swims in every day. You will love being in these waters; you will find solace, wisdom, courage and guidance as you accompany Joanne on her journey of loss—and renewal to the miracle that is life.

—Shira Nayman, author of Awake in the Dark, and Shoreline: A memoir of wandering, friendship and finding home

From a palliative care and bereavement perspective, this memoir fills an important gap. Many people struggle to articulate their grief, particularly adult children who are expected to "cope" and move on. This book offers language, recognition, and permission. It affirms that grief is not a problem to be solved but an experience to be lived, witnessed, and integrated over time'.

—Yvonne Coburn, formerly a National Champion for Palliative Care Australia

Written with unflinching honesty, grace, and love, I felt my own experiences of love and loss mirrored in Joanne's conflicted pull to be present for those suffering and yet the need to escape the claustrophobic wrench of dying.

—Jane Badler, actor and singer, Diana in NBC's science fiction series V

Bring Us Home From Sorrow is large of heart and narrative scope, traversing time and place, continents and generations. It moves vertically, into the depths of the narrator's inner world and back up to the exigencies of caring for a dying mother. This energy brings an extraordinary depth of generosity to the book – the quality of sharing that envelops the reader will provide many with profound consolation.

—*Katia Ariel, author of The Swift Dark Tide and The Ferryman*

Raw, wise and beautifully written, this is a book of rare emotional depth and grace. Joanne Fedler is a profoundly gifted writer, and *Bring Us Home From Sorrow* is luminous and life-affirming.

—*Jane Tara, author of Tilda is Visible*

Fedler writes this story as an arc through generations, meals, and memories. The arc becomes liquid; it reads like tides read gravity through the moon. You are called to swim through time and love the way mothers, daughters, sisters and entire cultures are brewed into being. Everything is here, and it is the water of life and death.

—*Nora Bateson, mother, daughter, award-winning filmmaker, President of the International Bateson Institute, founder and creator of Warm Data, author of Combining and Small Arcs of Larger Circles*

This book is a vigil for the secret life of grief. Written from inside the dark night of loss, it refuses to turn away from what is leaving, dying, or already gone. It is a love story, an ocean, a private room where devotion and absence kneel together. An extraordinary unveiling of the distances the heart must traverse, *Bring Us Home From Sorrow* offers a tender, brutal initiation into what grief knows about us.

—*Jessy Chapnik Kahn, poet, singer, author of MADRE*

Bring Us Home From Sorrow is a story of strong family bonds, love, loss and gratitude. It was as if I was reliving my beloved mum's passing through the eyes of another, and in doing so, I experienced a sense of healing. A beautiful read.

—*Monica Rosenfeld, Founder of Stories that Stir*

Bring Us Home from Sorrow is about steadiness and embodiment and the gentle ways we learn to survive loss. Through her practice of ocean swimming, Joanne shows how sorrow can coexist with beauty. This is a book that will touch you deeply.

—*Dr Linda Friedland, Medical Doctor and author*

This is one of the most beautiful books that I have ever read. I was allowed in the room as witness to the unravelling of the ties that bind a woman to her mother and the ways in which those ties are stitched back together in the processing of grief. Its pulse and life lies in Joanne's honesty and willingness to be so vulnerable. I read this book whilst grieving my own mother. It has been a tender balm in so many ways.

—*Liezel Graham, poet, author of* The Velveting Bones

Integrating grief is one of the most exquisitely difficult tasks of adult life. Fedler does not console or hurry past the raw ache of loss. Instead, she invites us to wade its watery depths, to discover the 'heaving, breathing, bountiful life' beneath.'

—*Hadass Segal, Psychotherapist and Swimmer*

PREFACE

On a chilly June morning in 2022, my husband Zed accompanies me into the city, first on a bus, then on a tram where we are enrolled to do a CPR course.

I need it to qualify as a trained swimming coach, a goal I've been working towards for nine months, because for a time, I fantasised that my life's purpose was to teach women how to swim, in a swim school called 'She Gets Wet.' It is the last outstanding item on a long and exhaustive list of requirements for certification, which I almost give up on half-way. But I am nothing if not a dogged finisher.

'But what do *you* need a CPR certificate for?' I'd asked Zed when he offered to do it with me.

'You never know when someone might have a heart attack right in front of you. And then do you want to be the useless schmuck who can't do anything but call 000?'

I'm happy for the company, especially if we're forced to pair up.

We eat a quick breakfast in the mall before making our way into the dank and cheerless building and standing in line with a group of strangers before the doors open for registration.

The instructor is a young woman, and it is clear from her tone that she has done this drill more times than any human should reasonably be asked to repeat the same thing and still give a fuck.

In a voice that does not betray how little she cares about the answer, she opens by asking the room full of people, 'Has anyone here ever done CPR on anyone?'

I look around. No-one raises their hand. And for a moment, it seems to me no-one will. Then I remember.

And with a shock, I raise mine.

I always swim alone.

It is not what they advise, 'they' being more experienced swimmers than I am, lifeguards, The World Open Swimming Association and anyone with decent common sense. Cramps, exhaustion, sudden rips, a gaggle of stingers, a heart attack and of course, sharks are all risks you take if you ignore the simple rule: never swim by yourself, regardless of your age or swimming level.

Why I choose to ignore this is as much a mystery to me as to you. Please don't try this at home.

It is a nippy autumn morning on Mother's Day 2022, and I bob through the whipping ripples and northerly gusts of wind, which sing in the high tide, raising me on the incoming swell in Coogee Bay, a beach in the eastern suburbs of Sydney. The rain-bulging clouds squat Sumo-like on the horizon. I'm taking a chance that the weather won't turn feral while I'm far from shore.

I'm a reasonably strong swimmer, but I know I am not drown-proof. Each morning, I make a calculated call about the conditions, and I never swim on an unpatrolled beach—but still, swimming alone is unwise, and it's part of what I like about it. Every time I venture out on my own, I am experimenting against my own nature, which for too long has been so catastrophically risk-averse. It is a lamentable, but unavoidable truth that I have deleted thousands of adventures from the possible story of my life. Enough of that.

I swim out a hundred metres or so from the shore. When I get to the northern end of the bay, in line with the three bronze interlocking bowed heads, the memorial sculpture to the 88 Australians who died in the Bali terrorist attack in 2002 (many of whom were Coogee locals), I lift my goggles onto my head and tread water, just to take it all in.

Beyond the arms of this bay, the sea stretches onwards in front of me. It is possible out here to spy wobbegongs, a species of non-aggressive carpet shark, which both terrify and thrill me; Port Jackson sharks, blunt and bull-headed, with brown and grey harness-like markings, also, to my recent amazement, harmless if you leave them be. More likely, I might chance upon a wrasse, bright blue if male, grey if female; stingray or skates along the seabed, or heavens, if luck is with me, a manta ray, black and eagle-like, a purple curtsying cuttlefish, an octopus hiding in rocky crevices; or the prize I have never spied in these waters, but I've heard other swimmers speak of, a turtle.

Out here, a sighting of any creature is a gift the ocean gives you. To encounter any being from this underworld, with its secret life, even for a moment, is to see a god. Most days, you will see nothing. This is part of the addiction to keep returning—on the off chance that today might yield a sudden meeting between you and a sea-homed animal. Just the hope of it sparks my blood.

Mother's Day has come to mean something different now, and my heart is tender as the tide lifts me and the rain threatens to cut my swim short.

Though I am swimming solo, I am not alone. I am surrounded by heaving, breathing, bountiful life. Beyond human gaze or eavesdropping, I wave to passing fish, call out to seagulls and cormorants and try to tail the groper whose territory is the north end of the bay. Here is my paradise. I can't remember who I was before I claimed this sanctuary.

It has not always been this way. But everything has changed.

I flip onto my back and call out to the sky.

If the dead are listening, out here might be the one place they can hear us.

PART 1
GOING BACK

CHAPTER 1

I am one of fourteen people on the plane.

There are just about as many air stewards as there are passengers, giving me a taste of what it would be like to have a personal butler. I find the endless check-ups invasive, pressing me for an ongoing chirpiness I cannot muster. From behind facemasks and transparent visors, stewardesses keep offering me bottles of water and increasingly unhealthy snacks. I'm allowed to remove my facemask to consume them, but as soon as I've swallowed, I must cover up once more. I am not a scientist, far from understanding how invisible catastrophes travel between people, but this seems random and imprecise. An unreliable protocol wrapped in a suffocating inconvenience.

I have made the flight from Sydney to Johannesburg more than twenty times in the past nineteen years since Zed and I immigrated to Australia with our two small children. The journey has always felt like a ruthless fourteen hours, just longer than seems tolerable to be wedged in stifling proximity to a stranger.

But now, in August 2021, at the height of Australian lockdown, Qantas isn't flying to South Africa, and no-one can say when international travel as we've always known it will resume. The skies have been emptied for months. This flight, via Singapore—my only option—is eleven hours off course to the north-west, then another ten, south-west back to Johannesburg. With three hours in transit, it is a full day to get to where I must be, in what makes absolutely no geometric sense. Fourteen hours now seems like a luxury. It is a long while to sit with a piece of fabric over my nose and mouth. Flying has always made me claustrophobic and panicky, even before respiration became a hazardous bodily function.

I do a few rounds of mindful breathing from behind my mask. *In for four, hold for four, out for eight.* A tranquilliser would be more efficient, and I'm not ruling it out if this doesn't work. I'm not against allopathic medicine—I'm only on this plane because I've had both my Covid vaccines; but given the choice, I prefer natural remedies, because I have something of a backstory wound when it comes to pharmaceuticals. I don't make a habit of holding grudges, but it is fair to say that I was overmedicated throughout my childhood for the smallest ailments, almost as if my mother was amassing loyalty points every time she put us kids on antibiotics.

Now that we have reached cruising altitude, and I am on my way, I can finally relax and unclench the tight fist of my nervous system. But eight months of anxiety sit in my bones. I am a mess of stress. I only feel the full brunt of it now that the frantic list of decisions and tasks to get me on this plane are behind me.

Leaving on any international trip always feels like a small kind of dying, invoking our mortality. When Zed and I went to Italy for three weeks a few years ago, we finally got our wills done and told the kids where to find them just in case… 'Could you just not?' our daughter Jess chided. 'Nothing is going to happen to you.'

She was right, nothing did. But someday it will. Then she'll be grateful for all that pre-disaster prep which can save a griever a great deal of time and bother. Some gratitudes we never live to witness.

Over the past few days, I marked in-the-event-of-emergency files for Zed and made some semblance of the chaotic order of my affairs including bank accounts, passwords, valuables and sentimental paraphernalia, should I be unable to point him in the right direction for any reason. I found it an exhausting exercise, exposing the disasters of my personality, habits and traits with hideous clarity. The mind is a quiet arrangement, entirely personal to the way we each make sense of the world. But I've done what I can.

At the last minute, I left post-it notes around the apartment.
CHANGE CAT LITTER ONCE A WEEK.
THIS IS FOR JESS (on specific books, clothes and jewellery).
BURN THESE DIARIES. DO NOT READ.

I cleaned out the fridge and the pantry knowing Zed won't venture near anything that needs finishing and dropped off boxes of perishables at my kids' homes in Kingsford and Newtown. My heart burned just to catch a glance of their eyes above their facemasks. I miss them to the point of physical pain. The empty nest plus Covid has been a brutal mathematics of loss. In the past days, Aidan registered with the NSW government to be Zed's 'support person' during my absence, just so he is allowed to visit him while I'm gone.

I am going to be in South Africa for three months, and not by choice. It's the longest I have ever been away since my twenties when I spent a year in the US doing a master's in law. But that was different. I didn't have a family. I wasn't a mother. I was heading out to grab life, not returning to grasp its final grains in the palm of my hand.

Three days ago, Zed brought down my blue suitcase from the cupboard and laid it on the bed. My packing muscles were slack, like withered limbs post-confinement. As I grappled with clothing decisions, baffled by the task as if it were a puzzle to solve without instructions, I wanted whatever was waiting for me on the other side of this trip to be over. Even before I left, I longed for the amnesty of a homecoming.

Now, I put my seat as far back as it goes and close my eyes. I am finally on my way, relieved we are past the pre-take-off performance simulating how to 'breathe normally,' into an oxygen mask in the unlikely event of a loss of cabin pressure—surely an outrageous ask amid an in-flight catastrophe? I always check to see if a life vest is, as they claim, under my seat and pray the day never comes when I will have to reach for it.

The anemone of my heart clenches as I remember that I didn't get to say goodbye to Archie—he was nowhere to be found in the rush before we left for the airport. These days I am certain of nothing but that it is criminal to leave the cat without explaining *I am going away but I will be back*. I made Zed promise he'd address my absence with him when he wanders back in for dinner.

We drove to the airport through eerily empty streets in what was once 'rush hour', making a quick detour at Jess's front door, where she pressed an envelope in my hand. *Only open it on the plane.* We hugged urgently, though that's technically against the social distancing rules.

'Send my love to Nana,' she said, tearfully.

The airport was deserted—not a car, taxi or passenger besides me. Two officials at Singapore Airlines greeted me by name, as if I were a celebrity or politician, someone for whom the waters part. I presented my exemption from the Australian government permitting me to travel, authorisation only granted on the strength of hard-hitting doctors' letters and affidavits. I showed my Covid vaccine certificates and the results of the overpriced Covid test from yesterday at a laboratory to prove I am currently not infected with the virus.

An official called Canberra. Confirmation. Permission.

'F-E-D-L-E-R,' he spelled into the phone, tapping his pen while he waited.

'What happens to people who don't have the exemption?' I'd asked.

'We can't let them fly. People try to get back to loved ones who are sick or dying, and if they don't have this paper…' he shrugged. 'We've seen some heartbreaking scenes.'

Loved ones.

That's what it boils down to now. Being with.

And the unbearable, intolerable, inhuman 'not-allowed's.'

While I'd stood waiting, I thought of the poor souls trapped in the Twin Towers or on those doomed flights on 9/11 who had made calls just to get the words *I love you* out one last time. It's only loved ones we think of when the plane is going down, or the cancer markers are going up. Even if these people annoy the shit out of us at Thanksgiving, Easter or Rosh Hashana gatherings. When we are facing the end, personalities, political opinions and the past become irrelevant. We find forgiveness we have never been able to muster during the good times. Why we need to be strung out to the edges in this way before we soften is one of the absurdities of our human condition.

I scanned the empty airport, a strange dread in my belly at the incongruity of finding myself in a real-life dystopian nightmare. My mother, father, sisters, niece, friends.

Distance from.

Can't get to.

Out of reach.

I was flying back to some loved ones, leaving others behind. Torn in half. What if I got stuck there? What if something happened to a loved one back here while I was away?

But I know how to switch off half of me. I did it once before when we immigrated. I could do it again. I fumbled for the dashboard inside me and felt all the lights shutting down. Zed. Jess. Aidan. Archie.

Alone in customs, I pulled out my iPhone with bemused wonderment to take a picture I would later post on Facebook; the caption would reference the deserted hotel in Stephen King's, *The Shining*, made into a horror movie with Jack Nicholson. A stern and humourless official suddenly appeared.

'You're not allowed to take photos in customs,' he snapped.

'Oops,' I apologised from behind my mask.

He demanded my phone, deleted the image and then deleted it from Deleted Items.

Hot tears pricked my eyes.

As he'd handed it back, I felt the edge of just how much erasure the human heart can bear.

A masked stewardess arrives with my meal asphyxiated in layers of plastic. I peel open the offerings to pick on the fruit.

I suddenly remember Jess's gift. I fumble and find it in my bag and tear open the large envelope containing a card with six pockets marked: *Flight There, Birthday, Late September, Late October, Flight Back and In Case of Emergency.*

The *Flight There* note reads, 'Know you are going exactly where you are needed, exactly where you should be and that love bookends your movements…. I will miss you.' I sob openly under my mask.

From my seat, I can see a middle-aged man some ten rows ahead and I wonder what urgency has thrust him on this flight. No-one here is travelling for pleasure, a safari or a romp around the Garden Route. Everyone is headed for a hard landing, flying at huge expense, having sliced through a forest of red tape because the prospect of not doing so is the stuff of which deathbed regrets are made.

But we are the lucky ones. I could not be more grateful to be on this plane, with all the costs involved, including two weeks in quarantine in a hotel room at my own expense. I've invested my life savings into this trip.

But as Zed said when I winced at the cost, 'This is the rainy day you've been saving for.'

I understood all at once, that we never ever want that rainy day to arrive.

CHAPTER 2

This is how the end began.

The first I knew of the disease that had invaded my mother's belly was a message she posted in the family WhatsApp group on 15 December 2020:

'Having blood tests and ultrasound. Have to see dr again afterwards. Not sure what is wrong.'

'What do you mean?' I texted. 'Ultrasound of what?'

'Have distended abdomen so came to see dr today.'

'Are you in pain?'

'No uncomfortable.'

I stared at the phone before typing the flaccid platitude:

'Sending you love, Mom.' I still called her 'mom' like we do in South Africa, though my kids call me 'mum'

An hour and fifteen minutes later:

'Not good news. Fluid in abdomen and cysts on ovaries. Waiting to hear from the dr.'

'What does it mean?' I asked in the first of what would become many useless desperate questions.

'May be ca ovaries.'

'Cancer of the ovaries?' My fingers trembled as I typed these words. *What was this some kind of doctor's shorthand?*

'-may be,' she wrote back.

My heart plummeted like an anchor.

The last time I saw my parents was eighteen months ago.

I'd just landed in South Africa to celebrate my mother's eightieth birthday when, days later, the world began to shut down. My travel agent had struggled to get me on a plane back to Sydney before the Australian borders closed. I promised we'd find a way to make it all up to her—the birthday celebrations with Zed and my kids whose flights had been cancelled. My sisters and I had cobbled a hasty makeshift party, a meagre version of the festivities we'd been planning, and presented her with a book of all her recipes, *What Shall I Make*? With loving messages from everyone in the family, a project we'd spent a whole year keeping a secret.

I told her I'd see her again before she knew it, this Covid thing would all be over in a heartbeat. She commiserated about me having to wear a face mask for the eleven-hour flight back. We agreed—such hysteria over a little virus.

I had taken a picture on my iPhone of my parents sweetly, sadly holding hands in the driveway, my mother in her bobbled pink fleecy waistcoat, wearing the new bright red slippers I had gifted her. This was how they had always stood, year after year, as I'd rip their grandchildren from their arms and ship them back to a faraway land where grandparents are forgotten. 'Keep them safe just like this until I can get back,' I prayed as the Uber swung out of the driveway that morning.

It is a year and a half since my naïve farewell, and we are only beginning to understand what Covid-19 is. Now part of the zeitgeist, this virus possibly spawned by a bat, has infiltrated and saturated us——literally and psychologically, consuming vigour, joy and tomorrow's plans. Our collective fear and anxiety have almost become their own strain of infection, as we test ourselves over and over again with swabs up the nose, to the back of the throat, waiting, watching for the two 'gotcha' lines.

We are living entirely in its thrall.

Though I speak to my mother most days, she hadn't mentioned her bloated belly—and when it comes to intimate bodily symptoms, our family is illiterate in the protocols of TMI ('too much information'). Now and then, there's a ping in the extended family WhatsApp group and what you'll find, ready or not, are up-close photos of someone's latest bruise, rash or suppurating wound. Zed still hasn't gotten his head around it.

As much as we all try to stay in touch, the reality of immigration means that I am not part of my parents' or sisters' daily lives. I cannot be there when they need me. I am peripheral, just out of synch, in a time zone eight and sometimes nine hours ahead. Despite WhatsApp updates, I miss out on day-to-day to-ings and fro-ings. Right here is where the lag happened. Crucial information had slipped through the cracks.

After a flurry of messages, I learned that my sister Carolyn, who is a medical doctor, had been nagging my mother to get her swollen belly checked out for a while. My mother, also a GP, dismissed it as nothing but a bit of extra Covid weight. She'd finally gone for an ultrasound, assuming her symptoms would reveal an easily treatable digestive condition. This right here is the nightmare we all pray never eventuates, where the ordinary turns to devastation.

Coldness slid into me like a long, deep needle as I tried to imagine my mother's fear. I added Jess and Aidan to the WhatsApp group with my sisters and mother. They always complain about too many notifications in our little family's WhatsApp group, but fuck it, this had suddenly gotten serious.

Of the three of us, my sister Carolyn is the most photogenic.

She is the eldest, and the one who can write you a script for tranquillisers, if necessary. She has also studied the longest—and not by choice. Born deaf, she was only diagnosed as hearing-impaired when she was two years old. My parents made the tough decision to send her to a school with hearing kids, rather than one for the deaf where she would have learned sign language. Carolyn spent every afternoon after school in speech and hearing therapy. With hearing aids, she now manages mostly by lipreading. She also surpassed every academic limitation prophesied by doctors and other doomsayers.

When she first applied, she was rejected by the medical school. They admitted her five years later, after she'd proved she could 'cope with university'—she'd aced her BSC and Honours degrees in Microbiology and Genetics, outshining peers who heard every word she had missed in lectures. Excelling in a world built to exclude you is one of my sister's many talents. She was the first deaf person to qualify as a medical doctor in South Africa and has been a senior chemical pathologist at a private pathology laboratory in Johannesburg for years.

It is always handy to have a doctor in the family, but when my mother was diagnosed, it became a blessing.

'Is it definitely cancer?' Laura had asked in the WhatsApp Private Sisters chat.

We non-doctors, what do we know? We need words like 'definitely.'

Carolyn: 'The op will confirm as the cysts need to be biopsied.'

I didn't yet know that this is how doctors ease you into terrible news. One laboratory report, one delay tactic at a time.

From the oncologist's rooms, Carolyn kept me and Laura in the loop via WhatsApp.

The plan was to drain the fluid in my mother's abdomen immediately to relieve the pressure, chemotherapy for three months to shrink the tumour bulk and only then, a big operation to remove ovaries, followed by three more cycles of chemotherapy. But before any of the cancer treatment, she needed a balloon valvoplasty to fix a faulty valve in her heart.

I had tried to keep up with all the information, but every new fact made my head hurt. All I could grasp was that my mother was very sick. I could barely hold the panic at bay. I felt the ice of it seeping into me.

Laura: 'So it's at advanced stage?'

Carolyn: 'Yes.'

Laura: crying face emoji.

From far away, I got on with my daily tasks—laundry, shopping, cooking, in a strange eerie haze, as a new sensation settled inside me. Every breath felt like a prickle, a thorn in my lungs.

Before we immigrated to Australia in 2001, I taught my mother how to use email. For the first few years, we corresponded with daily updates.

Then WhatsApp took over. She and I have been penpals though, since I was a child.

Whenever my folks went out at night, before bedtime, I'd write notes and leave them on my mother's bed. I'd ask about the movie or dinner party and tell her what we three sisters had gotten up to. These were the scripted equivalent of taking her face between my hands and getting her to look me in the eyes.

The following morning, there was always a folded reply next to my bed, like a gift from the Tooth Fairy. My mother responded to every one of my questions, never more than was necessary.

'A lovely movie.'

'Delicious food—beetroot soup with sour cream.'

'I didn't enjoy the loud music.'

Those notes were a tethering, a call and response, a way of managing my anxiety about her absence. I missed her even when she was close, sensing she was just about to disappear, like she often did in my recurring dreams where she'd drive off and leave me behind or was swallowed by the upstairs toilet. When I'd wake from bad dreams, I'd stand at the door to my parents' bedroom, trembling. My mother who was a light sleeper, was always annoyed at being woken.

'What's the matter?' she'd ask groggily.

'I've had a nightmare.'

'Just go back to bed,' she'd mutter. She'd never walk me back to my room or give me the hug I longed for. I'd return to my pillows, a big brave girl on her own, switch on my bedside light and reach for an Enid Blyton book. I'd imagine myself in a safe little world with a best friend who lived in a large mushroom or up the trunk of a magic tree who would never let me go off into the dark night on my own.

As a young teenager I began writing in journals, letters to a myself, where I asked questions about my life. What did things mean? I turned things over to shake out answers to my problems and anxieties. It became a habit I have kept up ever since.

On Tuesday 15 December 2020, I wrote in my journal: 'Mom diagnosed with advanced ovarian cancer. SHOULD I GO BE WITH MOM?'

From across the seas that divided us, over the next eight months, that question would twist inside me, helplessly, desperately.

Once again, I began writing letters to my mother, ones she would never read. This, right here, was the beginning of sadness.

I knew I was taking notes of the end.

CHAPTER 3

I accept another bottle of water from the air stewardess. What else is there to do over these long hours in the air but hydrate?

I put the time to use by freeing up storage on my iPhone. I scroll through the hundreds of texts and photos that have accumulated like cyberdust over the years. The past eight months are a nightmarish blur, but this catalogue marks each agonising foothold in a terrain that has the jagged and giddying geography of a snakes and ladders game.

I'd almost forgotten that two weeks after the cancer diagnosis, my father had flooded the upstairs by leaving the tap in the upstairs bathroom on. His terror had thrown him into an existential spin that was almost as hard to witness as my mother's suffering. He had floundered, literally drowning in his fear.

I find the exchange between me and my mother as she lay awake next to my sleeping father, worrying about all the things she had to do including getting the carpets changed.

I'd suggested she watch *Bridgerton* which I'd just finished bingeing.

'No, historically ridiculous.'

I'd found that funny given all the crap TV she loves to watch—reruns of *Judge Judy* and *Come Dine with Me* with that awful, irritating voiceover by Dave Lamb that drives my father mad.

In a complete non-sequitur, she went on to tell me she'd spent the day making chopped herring despite the terrible neuralgia in her hands brought on by the chemotherapy.

'Felt like cooking today as fingers not numb and tingling.'

'Such a good sign that you have an appetite, mama.'

'Dad is so upset about flooding; it was so unnecessary.'

'Shame, I feel for him. He's trying... in both senses of the word' (silly face emoji).

'He is taking a lot of strain. So worried about me and is so forgetful.'

'We all make mistakes and you are both under huge stress.'

'I know but he feels things so intensely,' she'd responded. 'Jo, dad is really frail these days but he's trying his best. Makes us coffee every morning. And Carolyn and Laura have been too wonderful.'

'I wish I was closer and could do more. I'm so grateful they're both there in your time of need. I'm so sorry I'm so far away.'

'Yes, I know.'

'It feels so wrong not to be right there with you now. Please forgive me.' I remember tearing up as I'd typed these words.

'Can't be helped.' And there she was, my practical, stoic, 'just go back to bed,' mother.

But when I'd had pneumonia during my second pregnancy she'd flown to Cape Town to look after me and help with the kids. I hadn't had to ask. She'd travelled to Australia years later when I needed a huge fibroid removed and was bedridden for a week.

'You have always been there for me,' I had texted. I had long ago forgiven her the inadvertent wounds of my childhood.

She did not respond to this message directly, instead she listed all the things she had to do. 'No wonder I can't sleep.'

I suggested she try guided meditations—there are lovely ones you can get on your phone for free.

'Not for me.'

I swipe back through my messages to her over the past months. She always responded, like she did with the notes I left on her bed as a child:

'Not good news.'

'Bit achey probably from chemo.'

'Horrible food but I ate it.'

'Having trouble sleeping.'

'Nauseous this morning.'

'Better appetite but that won't last.'

'Nice to talk to you.'

'Lot of pain today.'

'Waiting for blood results.'

'I really miss going shopping.'

'Very worried.'

'Thanks for long talk.'

'Horrible night.'

'Most of my hair has gone.'

'Very nervous.'

'Nothing to talk about.'

My mother uses words sparingly. Even her birthday cards are always confined to the simple, 'Happy birthday my darling, love mom.' Once she used 'ever-loving' and that slayed me.

I continue scrolling and stop at a photograph Carolyn had sent me the morning of our mother's operation just before they'd left for the hospital. My father is holding her hand. At the time, I could barely look at it. Something dark had entered me, slowly, unforgivingly, as if I was witnessing the moment before a ship sinks. But now, I pause. I try to be with this image, taking in the faraway look on my mother's face and the terrible terror in my father's eyes. Now, I see its tender beauty too.

Reading back, I remember there was talk of removing her bowel, depending on what they found when they opened her up, which meant the possibility of a colostomy bag. Yes, *whatever it takes*, I had thought, though I couldn't imagine how my proud, dignified mother would manage.

Blessedly, that hadn't been necessary. After the long and complicated operation, Theo, her friend and doctor had called me to say the operation had gone better than they could have expected. They'd removed the visible tumour bulk, and the microscopic malignancies would be 'mopped up' with chemotherapy. My despair had lifted like a migraine finally medicated, leaving me limp with relief. Surely it meant she was going to be okay?

'Mom, what wonderful news. We are all so happy. How are you feeling?' I'd texted her.

'Happy but uncomfortable. Having blood transfusion and catheter. Feels like bladder wants to explode.' Followed by an exploding head emoji, her terse simplicity embellished by a default auto prompt.

From her bed in the ward, we'd chatted about the terrible hospital food. Mushroom soup and custard. Dried out fish and mashed potatoes. She'd texted, 'Can't wait to get home, I am so sick of this place.'

That was my cue and I knew what to do. I had sent her a home-delivery menu so she could choose enticing dishes which I'd then had delivered to the house. When my mother had an appetite, we were in a world that made sense.

Back home, she'd tucked into the food I had sent her.

'Had roasted tomato soup last night and it was delicious.'

Now, as I read back over the texts, I see the fissures of her vulnerability. I notice that sometimes, I'd catch the right wave, and we were speaking the same language—it invariably involved food.

'I'm going to make mock crayfish and gefilte fish for Passover. Carolyn buying me fish tomorrow.'

'Hardcore, mama. How do you make it?'

'Mayo, tomato sauce, lemon juice, Worcestershire sauce, tabasco. It must have a kick.'

'What fish do you use, sounds delish,' I'd coaxed.

'Cook fish in a little lemon juice. Use kingklip and hake mixed. It can be very tasty. Gefilte fish is another story. Also Danish herring. Also used chilli and garlic salt. It's so frustrating not being able to go shopping. I really miss it. We're low on olive oil. Thanks for the long talk. Did you swim today?'

'I did, thanks, it was glorious as ever.'

'That's good. Sleep tightness

Right

Tight.'

I had done what I could from afar. I ordered bandanas for when her hair fell out. She'd asked for bright colours. I placed an order for the biggest box of bagels from Bagel Zone full of her favourite foods — smoked salmon, egg salad, pickles.

She'd responded with a line of heart emojis and a red telephone.

But even so, something dark and sinister hung over it all. I couldn't forget what my non-histrionic, quietly spoken medically trained mother had said when the biopsies came back, 'It's a death sentence.'

We lived from blood test result to blood test result. When the cancer markers rose from 54 to 67, I didn't know if this was terrible or not so bad, really. I didn't understand what anything meant and maybe I didn't want to. The superficial research I had allowed myself, painted a bleak picture. I googled Stage 4 ovarian cancer and then wished I hadn't. At times, the prognosis seemed clear, like Coogee Bay on a day when you can see the seagrass and vibrant blues of the water with pure clarity. Other times, I was caught in a murky haze of speculation and statistics, because goddammit, miracles also happen. I toggled between these vantage points, restless and unsettled. No matter where I stood, the disease was a landscape I could not escape. A new home I did not yet understand.

Over the months of her treatment, I would often lie awake through the night, with my hands over my belly, imagining the cancer in her ovaries. I tried to picture them—two pink jellyfish in the basin of her belly, which once jostled with miniscule eggs, one of which was half of going-to-be-me. Those little nuggets of genetic possibility were now haunted pods overrun by mutating malignant cells. What had once given life was now blossoming death. A stony knot of fear coiled behind my navel as I contemplated my own ovaries. Shouldn't I get those little ticking time bombs removed before this disease came to take me away from my children, husband, and life-as-I-know it, when I still have so much left to do on this earth?

More than once, she said, 'I brought this on myself,' 'I deserve it,' and 'I should have listened to Theo.' He had reminded her over the years to keep having her ovaries checked. I don't know why she never did. Hypochondriacs like me are better patients than that.

In my rational moments, I knew I had to prepare myself for the worst. I got hold of books on how to support dying people to have dignity to the end. To be fair, I've been reading books about dying all my adult life. But that was before anyone was dying.

I picked up Roland Barthes' *Mourning Diary* which he wrote after his mother died, as if I could study and prepare myself for what lay ahead. Barthes had not had a partner or children; his mother had been the centre of his world. He wrote of 'abandonitis'—the feeling of being completely deserted by all previous understandings of solace that involved his mother's presence in the world. His expressions of grief made me think, 'I'll be better at it than this.'

The moment it arrived, the cancer created a new world—not just inside my mother's abdomen, but in each of us tied to her, destabilising, seeping in to change everything. With Covid dominating our lives, it distressed me how irrelevant in the big picture, my mother's health was. She was eighty and had had a generous helping of years. But to me, my dad, sisters and her grandchildren, she was irreplaceable, and we couldn't imagine the world without her.

Sometimes, when I was swimming out in the salt blue sea, I would soften, accepting that the body must die of something. The heart will have its attack, the brain its aneurysm, the ovaries, their cancer. How else will we each come to our end? For all we know in some Akashic field beyond our conscious reach, our organs may vie to be chosen in sacred service to light our path into the great mystery beyond the flesh.

Still, I made an appointment to have my ovaries scanned.

When we land in Singapore, we are ushered off the airplane by officials in full Hazmat suits. We are marched in single file through the empty airport, with the appropriate social distancing, to a lounge where we must wait at tables spaced metres apart. *One person per table.* We are not allowed to mill about. Besides, there is no duty-free shopping or overpriced restaurants to distract us as we wait out the hours between flights—everything is shut down. We can order food from a brief menu. My Thai green curry arrives—a microwaved meal in plastic.

Our names are called as connecting flights are ready for boarding, and a designated official walks us to the gate, like a personal security guard.

I take surreptitious photos of this bizarre protocol. Someday soon, this will seem strange, won't it, when the madness subsides and the world returns to how it was?

In my early forties, I went to see an ophthalmic specialist after months of blurred vision, pain in my temples and searing headaches. I'd been keeping forensically detailed notes of my symptoms. It was obvious I had a brain tumour. I had done my research and had finally plucked up the courage to have my worst fears confirmed.

I wish I could tell you that this was the first time I'd imagined my time was over. But I've been afflicted with dying thoughts for as long as I can remember. As a child, I suffered from frequent headaches and sore throats. My mother gave me sheets of pain relief tablets to keep in my pencil case so I could self-medicate because she couldn't keep picking me up from school when I wasn't feeling well. Her bathroom cupboard was crammed with pills pharmaceutical reps offloaded onto her, which she, in turn, offloaded onto us. No-one ever thought to ask whether the cause of a headache was physical (dehydration? a virus?), emotional (heartbreak?) or spiritual (what's-the-meaning-of-life?) By the age of ten, I'd had five operations for various ailments and developed a full-blown terror of doctors, hospitals and getting cancer.

On that day, in the ophthalmic surgeon's room, I removed a notebook from my bag and was about to launch into a detailed description of my symptoms.

'That won't be necessary. We'll do the standard tests and see what's going on.' He began to set up a machine.

This annoyed me. I had kept daily notes of every pain, throb and spasm. I had a list, the painstaking work of weeks of self-observation. What sort of physician dismisses a patient's careful list? I was helping him with my diagnosis.

He did a routine check-up. He got me to push my face up against a machine and look through apertures where lights flashed. I scrutinised his every movement from the way he wrote his notes, held his pen, and adjusted his glasses to see if his body language had 'brain tumour' coded in them, and he was preparing to tell someone some very unfriendly news.

He cleared his throat.

'Ms Fedler,' he paused, 'you have all the signs of someone in need of reading glasses.'

I broke all medical protocol, rushed over to his side of the desk and gave him a huge hug. I think I dislodged his glasses as I burbled, 'I am just so relieved, thank you, thank you, thank you.'

I had called Zed on my way out.

'I don't have a brain tumour, I don't have cancer,' I sobbed.

'Congratulations. I'm so proud of you,' he said.

Now I don't share this story proudly. Writing it down has only made it seem even more ridiculous. But for most of my life, this is how it has been for me. It has always taken a very small symptom for me to conjure up my own funeral.

Yes, laugh away. Zed does it all the time. Once, he watched me nurse a bleeding nose with a look of panic in my eyes and, without a trace of compassion, muttered, 'There's no such thing as nose cancer, you know.' Which, by the way, he is completely wrong about. I Googled it, and let me tell you, nasal cancer is no joke. But as Zed says, 'There's no cure for no-cancer.'

Over the years, I've variously tortured myself with imagining I've got bowel cancer, breast cancer, brain cancer, intestinal cancer, thyroid cancer, cervical cancer, uterine cancer, melanoma and pancreatic cancer (and that's just the cancers—let's not forget ALS and brain aneurysms). I've been through endless cycles of 'tests' to see which organ has turned on me this time, and how much time I've got left, seeking doctors' opinions, convinced I'm about to be told 'eat as much ice cream and chips as you like, and say your goodbyes.'

A friend once told me that I would attract cancer with all the energy I gave to my anxiety. This only amplified my fears. He is the same friend who gave me a copy of *The Secret*, so apparently, if life did not dish out cancer to me as part of my destiny, I would manifest it because I spent so much time fretting about it. My yoga teacher said it more kindly: 'Worrying is like praying for things we do not want.'

I've spent decades and have invested time, money and effort in searching for ways to take charge of the 'Animal Farm' of my thoughts. I'm glad to report that I have made progress. But this news about my mother shook me backwards. We never know what disasters are fermenting in the dark cocoon of the body or what perverse anarchy Nature has let loose, unseen. Without defending health-anxiety as a life choice, I wondered whether my mother's cancer wasn't proof that fear is sometimes justified.

But something changed that day as I skipped out of the eye doctor's rooms, relief swishing through my veins. I was finally sick of circling this same spiral of fear, terrified of everything—not just disaster, but happiness and success too. I'd even managed to infect joy, mistrusting it as a prequel to tragedy.

Though I had bargained my way out of every imaginable death-sentence up to that point, and celebrated each birthday with a huge sigh of *I made it here,* fear and its army of minions had dominated my life, motivating all my decisions ('No thanks, I won't have a go on the kayak, the water looks a bit rough'; 'We'll take a raincheck on camping, there might be snakes and spiders'; 'I'd rather not be in a remote place where there are no hospitals'). It had distorted the kind of person and parent I became—someone terrified of all the what-ifs in the world, never able to trust the universe.

I had read enough about neuroplasticity to realise we can unwire core beliefs. I knew I had to break the loop, not only for my mental health, and poor long-suffering Zed, but to make sure I didn't burden my children with my neuroses.

I went to therapy and annual meditation retreats. I read dozens of books on being sick and dying, including classics by Louise Hay, Caroline Myss, Gabor Mate, Stephen Levine and Stephen Jenkinson. I began to feel kindly towards my pathetic self and soothed her, like a mother might, a nightmare-stricken child. Over time, I got stronger so that I could go for mammograms, pap smears and other checkups, without needing a tranquilliser to get me there. The real test came one year when I got called back from a routine mammogram for 'further tests.'

I counselled myself, 'If it is breast cancer, how lucky am I that they found it early?'

Fear began to fade like an old photograph. Therapy helped. Every long, silent meditation retreat smoothed out my snagging mental burrs. I presented myself at the Red Cross to give blood because only healthy people are eligible to donate. I began to ease myself away from a cliff's edge in my mind.

I became curious to understand where my anxiety came from and started to research intergenerational trauma. After reading Mark Wolynn's book *It Didn't Start with You,* I realised women on both sides of my ancestral line had been stricken with illness and died young.

Families, I saw, are not made up of individuals but are more like cells in a living ecosystem which share not only DNA, but narratives, phobias and hauntings. What happens to one of us, happens to us all. What injuries one suffers, hurt everyone. And perhaps, the healing of one might offer relief to all.

In the movie *Twelve Angry Men*, one juror sways an entire jury from a verdict of guilty to not guilty, one person at a time. A single calm leader can soothe a broken community. Family constellation work is built on the idea that one individual who is willing to feel the pain carried down from the previous generations can heal the soul of an entire family system.

As I settle into my second flight, I'm nervous about how much I want this—grasping is never a good sign—to prove that I can be that person for my family.

CHAPTER 4

Now and then Zed and I find ourselves in a semi-serious exchange about who needs to die first. We debate who might cope better alone and the sequence that would be the most financially beneficial to those left behind. Given Zed's meticulous record-keeping and how rarely he frequents the headquarters of his feelings, he'd probably cope better with grief and the practicalities. But as I do most of the emotional labour, I'd likely be more of a support to the kids. It seems, therefore, something of a hypothetical tie.

In my parents' case, there has never been such competition. No-one has ever questioned that my mother would be the last parent standing, and dodder into her nineties. It was always my father's job to die first.

My mother oversees all the accounts, pays the bills, knows every password, does all the grocery shopping and cooking, arranges all the meals, is up to date with the insurance, the banks, the wills, the unit trusts, the lot. She has been the concierge, maître d, accountant, events manager, chef, and general dogsbody who has always held my father's world together.

My dad is in charge of making people laugh. That is his job and his superpower. Though he was one of South Africa's leading political cartoonists for fifty years and can zap out an incisive punchline in a blink, he can never find his glasses, which are invariably perched on his head. He's never missed a deadline. For years he churned out five leader page cartoons a week for *The Star* newspaper, but is always losing his keys, phone and wallet, which he could swear he put down just here, or maybe there, or in the car or next to his bed, and would you mind, while you're up, just going upstairs to look? Over-indulged and cared for by women all his life, like many male artists, he has elevated the art of learned helplessness to pioneering peaks.

A few months after flooding the bathroom, he had a terrible fall and was bruised black and blue.

Sometimes, he'd weep on the phone to me in private, 'What's going to happen to me? I can't do anything for myself.' He was overwhelmed by the prospect of the mundane practicalities of running that big house—switching on the oil heater in the loungeroom, changing TV channels and arming the house with the alarm, all of which I assured him he could learn.

'I've been spoiled, mollycoddled…' he confessed.

My mother had looked after him like an overgrown toddler for close to sixty years.

'Don't write her off just yet,' I told him. 'You can always die first.'

'I'm trying,' he said.

He'd made some valiant attempts over the years; his most spectacular one was in December 2018 when Zed and I were housesitting for a friend in the beautiful village of Maleny in Queensland. My father had been hospitalised for a routine bladder flush for a cancer he'd managed to keep under control for many years. But things had gone wrong during the procedure. He was slipping into organ failure.

Come now, Carolyn said.

As a migrant, you know to expect these calls. The diligent among us set aside special savings accounts for emergencies and funerals.

It was a scramble to get from Maleny to Brisbane, Brisbane to Sydney and Sydney to South Africa. But within thirty-six hours, I was at his bedside in ICU, where I found him tentacled to machines in a semi-conscious state. But as I left the ward, I was speared with pain down my left thigh. An MRI a few days later revealed a severely prolapsed disc in my lower back. For the next eight weeks, I couldn't stand or walk and was consumed with the kind of physical agony from which I pray you and everyone you love will be spared.

What a failure. I'd come to help my mother, to be her driver to and from the hospital, her feeder to make sure she ate three times a day, the holder of her hand, the emotional support person to *her* while we waited to see if my father was going to live or die. I ended up being a liability, another person she had to take care of while my dad slowly clawed his way back from the brink. I watched the strain gouge her face as she looked after two invalids.

During the weeks my father was in hospital, she and I slept side by side. We held hands and spoke long into the night. In this sacred space between worlds, cracks open up between people who have had a lifetime to tell each other the most important things and yet, never have, until now. Words find their slithery way, like water seeping through hairline fractures. All the losses and absences I'd felt in my childhood fell away. It was the most tender time between us, ever.

I've often reflected that perhaps I had come back just for those dark hours with my mother in which something between us was sealed, healed.

My mother says that when I was little, she could never get me out of the water on our family beach holidays. I have vague memories of losing a sense of time when I was in the ocean and then, whimpering at night, as she rubbed aloe vera on my back and face, sunburnt to a crisp from hours in the surf. Perhaps I stopped swimming when I was a teenager, and the scrutiny of wearing a bathing suit was too much to bear. It was Zed who taught our kids to swim in the sea, while I'd wait on the sand, ready to wrap little people in towels. On sweltering days, I'd go for a dip, never putting my head underwater or going further than where my feet could touch sand.

It is so easy to forget what we love.

But if we're lucky, something reminds us of what we've lost and invites us to make the strange, familiar again.

When I arrived back in Sydney after two months on my back, I'd hobbled down to the ocean bath below the Surf Lifesaving Club at the south end of the beach, to move the maimed mule of my body. In the water, the granite of my limbs lightened, and my spine was absolved of the battered burden of me. Held and free to kick and twirl, I floated. The song of the sea that lived inside my bones from my childhood returned and slipped me back into the cetacean skin of my animal self.

Over the weeks, I advanced to a few gentle laps. When I could manage thirty minutes in the water with ease, I looked out over Coogee Bay beyond the walls of the enclosed baths and watched swimmers make their way across, north to south end, their strokes strong and sure and fearless, against the pulsing blues of light and sea and sky. It looked so damn sexy and free.

Could I ever do that?

My hunger for the open water and who I might become if I could ever face that liberating vastness grew irresistible. I lusted, not in a virginal sense, but with reawakened sexual desire, a pining for something I had been missing, someone I had once been, but had abandoned.

Three months after my L5 S1 disc prolapsed in a hospital corridor across the ocean, I stood waist-deep in the bay, my heart jangling with adrenalin; before I thought too hard about what I was about to do, and talk myself backwards, I pushed off the ocean floor and swam beyond the breakers, where I did not yet know, the greatest love affair of my life awaited.

For the past three years, I have stood each day on Coogee beach and scanned the surface of the ocean, looking for rips, patches where no waves break. That's where the water pulls out to sea. Depending on the conditions, I sometimes I want to glide into that current and be carried out beyond the breakers where I am the only human speck bobbing on the surface. To get back, I must escape that narrow slip stream and swim into the flow that pulses the waves to the shoreline. Every day, hour by hour, the map of the terrain changes, as high tides contract to low tides; winds change, swells rise and fall, and the moon's cycle shifts and shuffles the topography I think I know so well.

Whenever I venture out, I am giving myself to the ocean.

Each time I return to shore, the ocean gives me back to my life.

I dare forget the grace of this arrangement.

I swam daily, until I grew strong, my breathing patterns lengthened, modified strokes gave me lilt and glide; and swim by swim, my fear of cold water, waves, rips, bluebottles and sharks faded. I got stung, once, twice, three times. I was dragged by majestic rips and learned to swim out of them. A time came when I was ready to face the 2.4km swim around Wedding Cake Island, 800 metres off the shore of Coogee beach, with hundreds of strong swimmers who all left me behind. But still, I finished.

'I don't know how you did that,' Zed beamed, when I stumbled back onto the beach, breathless and buzzing with adrenaline.

My parents, on the other hand, could not have been less excited by the news of all the ways I was choosing to conquer my fears.

'What about the sharks?' my father had asked, while I was on speakerphone. 'Aren't you scared?'

'Dad, of course I'm scared,' I told him. 'It would be foolish to swim in the ocean without understanding I'm only a guest. But it would be worse to not do it, because the chances are, it will be okay, more than that—it will be magical.'

'Oh Joanne,' I heard my mother sigh. 'What for?'

During the long months of lockdown, as the days blurred into sameness and time became meaningless, I never missed a morning down at the beach for sunrise with my towel and goggles. The fulcrum of my waking hours became the half an hour of outdoor exercise that the government permitted us, the way the arrival of a newborn rearranges priorities, sleeping patterns and life goals.

In the first few weeks, the beach was cordoned off, the benches red-taped; the steps barricaded. Masked officials marshalled us up and down entry and exit pathways. Over loudspeakers, lifeguards repeated that we were to return home once our workout was done. In amplified proclamations, we were reminded that if we dallied in the sun, gathered in groups for chit-chat instead of for cardiovascular purposes, or god forbid laid our *tuchuses* down without doing sit-ups or push-ups, the entire privilege of the outdoors, the gift of spending time in nature, would be taken from us and the hatches of the seaside would be battened down. The beach would be closed.

I was fastidious about sticking to the rules because I knew that the tentative nest of my mental health rested entirely on those salty immersions. As long as I could stride into the water, feel the slap of the waves against my belly and sink my face beneath the surface, I knew I could get through another day of whatever the hell was waiting for us in the next news report. In the tug of the ocean's muscle, as I concentrated on my breath, timed a stroke with a nudging swell or let a rip sail me out on the south end towards McIver's Ladies Baths, I was part of something bigger than the contracted world of Covid regulations.

Once, a huge school of huge silver fish—hundreds of them—formed a sequined vortex around me. Some days, I came across the male groper at the north end of the bay, radiant with the kind of blue that makes you believe in colour as an anti-inflammatory for the soul. Out there, I felt so small, I could disappear, and the calamity that was swallowing my world took its place in the vastness of all life.

While my mother was having chemotherapy, losing her hair and fighting for more time, I swam and swam and swam.

Emma was my first Australian friend—I'd met her just days after we'd immigrated at the childcare centre at a gym my mother insisted I join, just to get some time to myself each day. She had a way with kids and could be both wistfully fairylike and sternly rule-enforcing. She soon became our babysitter and one of my dearest friends, despite our ten-year age difference. She was finishing her nursing degree, a profession she'd been called to pursue after she'd been on a bus when it struck a young woman. Emma had held her hand and comforted her until an ambulance arrived. The next day, she called the hospital only to be told the young woman had died. Right then, she decided she wanted to become a nurse.

Many years later, we were sitting at a sushi train, and as the seaweed salad and salmon sashimi rolled past us in an endless loop, she told me that she had a premonition she was going to die young.

And you know what I did? I laughed. I took both her hands in mine and said, 'My darling, there is no reason in the world for you to die young. You are being totally ridiculous.'

'It's just a feeling,' she said.

'I think I'm dying all the time,' I reassured her.

Within months, three people I knew had died from Covid. The horror of it floated on my consciousness like the Great Pacific garbage patch out in the middle of the ocean, unabsorbable. Out there, in some shrouded future, the ruins of our lives beyond this horror beckoned.

While we waited for a vaccine, I berated myself. Fuck it, why hadn't I become a pandemiologist? I'd aced biology at school. I could draw a spirogyra like nobody's business. Why did I choose language over laboratories? What a waste of a good brain. I had no useful skills now, when the world needed them.

My years as an expert in domestic violence, in which I'd set up a legal advocacy centre and sat on a South African Law Commission to draft new legislation, had not prepared me for the day when women would be forced into isolation with their abusers. It felt like a gargantuan failure of imagination on my part, naivete mistaken for optimism about just how far from 'normal' normal could become.

I worried about the generation of youngsters losing important milestones in their psychological and social development, like final years at school and first years of university. I read articles about kids completely retreating into the online world—their only tether to social life—and predictions about the disastrous impact it would have on their interpersonal skills and mental health in years to come. I sensed that crucial immune-boosting ingredient of life—hope—slipping away. Zed stayed up all night watching the 2020 Olympics, distracting himself with gold medals and Australian sporting triumphs. I tried to engage him in the big philosophical questions and get his take on how long he thought the lockdown would continue. 'I don't know, this is my first pandemic,' he shrugged.

Now and then, I remembered that the tentative dreaming, cautious planning and deep impermanence of this time were trustworthy ingredients of a spiritual journey. I reminded myself that monotony could be a powerful teacher. Who were we to imagine we were ever in control of anything? All I could do was sentinel my own precious sanity. I have never felt as acutely as I did then that, as the spells of human sovereignty over nature were being broken, everything we already knew as a civilisation was a trap, and something unknown was emerging from the wildness. When I swam, I sensed the water was the healthiest it had ever been in all the years I'd been swimming, so full of life—bursting with clown fish, little silver and purple darts of light, bream, pufferfish, and gropers. Maybe this was a chance for the world to reset itself.

Each day, I tried to find a holy instant in the smothering sameness of the mundane.

I often found it in the water where I whispered words of prayer and thanks.

Help us to find a vaccine.
Please let the chemotherapy kill the cancer.
Comfort my mother in her fear.

I binged on nature documentaries and light, warm series like *The Durrells* about the British naturalist Gerald Durrell's childhood on the Greek island of Corfu. At the end, his widowed mother Louisa has to return to England because of the war, after having waited years for Spiros, a married man, to finally be free to be with her. But Spiros cannot go with her, for it would mean abandoning his children. Eventually, in each other's arms, realising a future together was not possible, she asks, 'What was it all for? All the waiting and the longing?'

And he says, 'Would you have missed it if you'd known?'
Those words undid me.

At the suggestion of my Buddhist teacher Joyce, I read the diaries of a young Dutch Jewish writer, Etty Hillesum, written between 1941-1943, who died in Auschwitz at the age of 29. She believed the only way to survive the atrocities of the outer world was to cultivate inner peace. When she was taken to Westerbork labour camp, she'd taken one book with her, a companion through the darkest hours, Rilke's *Book of Hours*. So, I too read Rilke.

I wondered whether, as a culture, we would grow while we were, in his words, 'being defeated… by ever greater things'?

I thought of my mother, being ambushed by microscopic cancer cells, but could feel no salvation in that, only defeat.

In the midst of all this turmoil, my daughter fell in love.

I couldn't wait to tell my mother that Jess was bringing her new partner for dinner. Being her first grandchild, they've always had a special bond.

'Lovely, what are you making?' she wanted to know.

I outlined the menu in the kind of detail she loved to hear.

'Sounds terrific.' She is the only person who ever used that sweet old-fashioned word, 'terrific.'

Later, she messaged me, 'How was supper? Longing to hear.'

This is what life is. During this heartbreaking time, Jess glowed, radiant with happiness. It was so confusing.

CHAPTER 5

After so long in the air, I can't tell whether I'm hungry, thirsty, tired or anxious. My body is scrambled with circadian discombobulation. With just a few more hours to go before we land, I suddenly realise I don't know what to expect when I arrive. This whole drama has played out over WhatsApp for me. What will it be like to have my mother within arm's reach?

She has been stoic and tight-lipped throughout, except once, when she flailed on her 81st birthday.

My sisters and I had tried to spoil her with roses, cards and sushi I ordered from Uber Eats, which she'd tucked into, with a fragile smile, bald as a little chick, all her hair gone. But sometime during the day she'd had a breakdown and cried. The backlog of emotions had breached her almost immaculate defences.

My father's hand-drawn birthday cards are legendary, the highlight of every celebration. But he hadn't made her a card. He hadn't even wished her a happy birthday. Carolyn had taken him aside and berated him. He confessed that he couldn't muster the effort to be humorous.

'A card doesn't have to be humorous, just an acknowledgement of a special day,' Carolyn countered. Chastised, he'd trundled upstairs to his study and returned with a hasty drawing and message.

'How was your birthday?' I texted during the day.

'I had a big cry in front of everyone. I am not a crying person so was embarrassed but couldn't help it,' she confessed.

In a way, I was relieved.

'You don't have to be embarrassed—you have cried so little in your life. You have lots of crying vouchers you've never used,' I responded.

We enumerated how many more chemo sessions to go.

'Every day feels like a week,' she typed.

'I want to know how you're really feeling. You can cry with me,' I tried.

'It's hard for me to cry.'

'I know, but you just need to practice,' I added three silly face emojis. 'Is there anything you need that would help or support you? Do you want to talk to a therapist?' I asked, though I knew the answer.

'No thanks.'

'I am cross with Dad.'

If there is any moment that sums up who my mother was as a wife and human being, it was her reply:

'Don't be cross, he is very upset.'

'He should be thinking about you, not himself,' I responded.

'No, he is upset about me and it's good for him to do this work on *Gagman* with you,' she said, referring to a project I was helping him finish, a graphic novel he'd been working on for thirty-five years.

A few weeks before, Carolyn and I had had a secret conversation. As the doctor, she was my mother's support person. She was taking her to every appointment, consulting with the medical team and driving her to and from chemotherapy. Laura had taken over managing their finances and affairs. But Carolyn asked for my help in handling my father. I was relieved to have a concrete job, even from afar. Since then, Zed had taken to calling me the 'rodeo clown,' as I diverted my father's attention with rewrites and creative input into this story he'd been working on for decades about a Jewish man in the concentration camps who survives by telling jokes to the Nazi commandant.

Every day, I called my dad to discuss his novel. I edited the manuscript, made structural suggestions and rewrote whole sections. My father was ecstatic with what I'd done with it, sensing his life's work wouldn't die unfinished. It brought us closer at a time when my patience with his endless attention-sapping accidents was threadbare. After months of forensically working through the many drafts and piecing the narrative together, I sent a draft for my mother to read.

'You are a genius,' she wrote back. In some ways, she was just like every other Jewish mother.

I sent it to my literary agent, and when he emailed to say he wanted to represent *Gagman*, my father was thrilled. To me, it was a limp, colourless joy, belonging to a lost world where these things had once mattered.

During the early years of our immigration, I had managed the missing of my South African family in cycles of homesickness and slow numbings. Little by little, I learned to live without them, and they got on with their lives without me. Zed often said, 'Sometimes your mother looks at me with such sadness in her eyes. I think she blames me for taking you all so far away,' an observation I have always refuted. I was sure she was glad we'd left South Africa and were raising our kids in Australia. But over the past months, when the distance I always claimed was 'just a fourteen-hour flight away,' proved untraversable, guilt and defeat had set in my bones like concrete. It was wrong to be so far away, a misunderstanding not only of place but of purpose.

A friend who had lost her mother to ovarian cancer reminded me that my mother still had much to teach me. 'Lean in,' she encouraged. I tried. From across the seas, I burrowed deep into the work of what a terminal illness in a family calls on each of us to take on. But with each passing treatment, my mother said less and less, her fear detectable only in a tremble in her voice, in her short, terse answers to my endless messages. Once when I texted her after a blood test result, she simply replied, 'Don't feel like talking.'

Now and then, I recognised the gifts distance gave us. For one thing, I was always awake in Sydney to receive her texts during her loneliest hours through the night. Here was a reversal of our roles—I could be there for her when the darkness claimed her. I had the chance to compose myself before we spoke. On the other side of a WhatsApp call, I listened quietly. I hid my fears and wept in private.

During one of our face-to-face conversations, she began to cry. I had only ever seen her weep once before—after her father died. When I was fourteen, it was a shocking disfiguration of the mother I knew. But on this occasion, it was a breakthrough.

'It's okay mama, you can cry. You don't have to protect me,' I said. She nodded.

'What is your worst fear?' I asked. I hoped she would say something that would allow me to rest a hand on her trembling heart.

There was a pause as she composed herself. I waited, hopeful. But all she said was, 'I don't like talking about it—it upsets your father.'

I don't know when exactly, but I began to slowly know the disease would take her, both too quickly for the heart and too slowly to witness, and I knew there was nothing left for me to do—no fixes, solutions or ways out of this final destination. It was just a matter of time before I would become a child again, wailing against a story without a happy ending.

My eyes are bleary after three movies, and my back aches. I venture to the loo, walking the barely populated aisles. I make eye contact with one of the other passengers. I smile, but unless she can see it in my eyes, how could she tell? In the toilet cubicle, I remove my mask and inhale deeply. I wash my puffy face and brush my furry teeth. I have no idea what time of day my body thinks it is. Before I put my mask back, I stare at the person in the mirror. Something has changed.

The thing Zed always said about my mother's eyes—I see it in mine now.

CHAPTER 6

My mother doesn't believe in God.

This is the thought that's bothering me as I look out the window while we fly towards the smoggy dawn of a Johannesburg morning.

My father is the resident mystic, who's hitchhiked his way through yoga, kabbalah and orthodox Judaism, a pilgrimage my mother has staunchly tolerated as the outfits, regalia and rituals have morphed. Of the two of them, he's the one who believes in miracles, my mother, only in chemicals.

In this way, I am more my father's daughter. I've always felt a greater presence, something I call God, though I'm not attached to labels. I'm just as happy addressing it as 'Life,' 'Spirit,' 'Shekhinah,' or 'Shirley.' It comforts me to whisper my fears into the Great Silence or address God in my journal when I am floundering. Frankly, I have never understood how atheists sustain the whole shlep of their lives without a belief in something beyond the ego and body-self.

Long before my mother's diagnosis, I had worked towards a tentative understanding that death is not a trespasser who has the *chutzpah* to show up in our lives uninvited. Nor is it a stranger we can palm off on the bouncer to deal with, *I'm sorry, but your name is not on the list*; a hovering presence beyond our locked gates on whom to set the guard dogs.

Remember how that went down with Siddhartha Gautama, a prince born into privilege and wealth? For the first sixteen years of his life, his father kept him barricaded inside a palace to buffer his son from a confrontation with sickness, old age and death. Until one day, the prince found himself in the village and came upon a sick old man, in the throes of dying. He had no frame of reference for what he saw. I imagine this encounter as a heightened version of discovering late in life that you are, in fact, adopted, and everything you previously thought about yourself has been fiction. Privilege is just this—ideological airbags in a collision with brutal reality.

The shock of this late onset awareness inspired the prince to throw off his robes and go in search of 'the truth' about life. He starved himself within an inch of his own death. He sat under a tree for longer than anyone wants to sit under a tree. Until he got it. When he stood up and walked clear of the shade of the Bodhi tree, he understood how to end human suffering and devoted himself to teaching so the rest of us can wake from the anesthesia of our denial.

The kernel of his discovery was this: death is not 'out there.' It is much closer than that. It is our destination from the moment we are born. 'The first breath is the beginning of death,' goes the proverb. There are no special business class lines and secret corridors for the rich, famous or extremely good-looking. It's the mortal version of that Japanese kids' book by Taro Gomi, *Everyone Poops*.

Yet for the most part, we live our lives with our backs turned against this knowledge. Perhaps if we held the tender surety of our demise as fervently as we held our political opinions or even our Netflix preferences, we may suffer less. Life is suffering, the Buddha taught, but to suffer over our suffering, is what he called 'The Second Arrow.' One is surely enough.

Even if the Divine is nothing more than a projection of my

imagination, and there really is nothing out there but stars and sky, being open to the possibility that death is not the end, has changed the way I live.

Once, on a meditation retreat, I was told I had twenty minutes left to live. When the bell rang, I was going to die. It was a Meeting Death exercise, but still, I had raced outside into the sunshine clutching my diary, ripped out a page and scribbled a note to Zed telling him he had been the love of my life. I told him to run as much as he could, love again, take care of the kids and the cat, light my lanterns, and remind the kids that God is everywhere even though it has never been clear to me that Zed believes in God. It was a clumsy message—but my time was running out.

Then I scrawled a letter to the kids telling them they had been the gifts of my life. I asked them to take care of their dad and each other. I told them to live their lives, find their passion and chase it, like 'it's the last bus of the night.' I plagiarised that from quotation anthologist Terri Guillemets, but really, as I was about to perish, I could not worry about being original.

Once these notes were written, the panic subsided. A strange and eerie calm settled in me. It was done. My life was over. The laundry, the to-do lists, taxes, orgasms, worrying about cancer, tsunamis, belly fat, terrorism, whether the kids would be safe. It was all finished.

I was tearful, but surprisingly, not sad. There was a strange elation to it all.

Back home, when I relayed the experience to my family, my kids thought it was dumb. 'But you knew you weren't really going to die,' Aidan had said.

'Well, not right at that moment, but I felt in my body that I will die—someday. It was just an imaginative exercise.'

'Why would you want to pretend you're going to die?'

'To practice.'

He'd shrugged.

'You wouldn't want to go into an important basketball final without training, would you?'

'Yeah, but that's different.'

Every day, Zed heads out for a run to prepare for the occasional marathon or ultramarathon. I've put in more than ten thousand hours at a keyboard, so I can publish a book every couple of years. Eating during famine depends on how well we've hoarded in times of plenty. Likewise, we can only draw on serenity in a crisis if we have made a habit of inviting it into our hearts during the lulls. This is surely the purpose of all the spiritual work we do over a lifetime. Every act of mindfulness, each affirmation or prayer is a soul sit-up. Navy Seals, firefighters and paramedics perform their drills. Musicians practise scales daily. All this training wires neurons and builds muscle memory, so when the big moment comes, we know what to do. To have grace under fire, we must stockpile it beforehand, like we've been doing with toilet paper through Covid.

I lean back in my seat now and try to feel the swell behind me, the heft and depth of the reservoirs I have been gathering inside me: all my years of Buddhist contemplation, annual silent meditation retreats, therapy, breathing exercises, and mantras, including the Three

Remembrances of the Buddha:

I am of the nature to grow old.
I am of the nature to get sick.
I am of the nature to die.

But something afraid flutters in me, like a scarf snagged on a nail in the wind. All the languages of consolation I know rely on a spiritual grammar and the semiotics of transcendence.

I've been watching on helplessly as my mother flounders. It saddens me terribly, this sense that it might be too late for her to find comfort in the part of herself she doesn't believe in, but I know is there: her soul.

In his thirties, the poet Mark Nepo survived lymphoma which had spread to his brain. He went on to defy medical science and make a complete recovery from his terminal illness, leaving doctors baffled. When asked what contributed to his healing, he said he couldn't point to any one practice or intervention. All he could suggest is that he'd not been attached to any single 'cure,' but had embraced the whole lot—every blessing, ritual, shamanic spell, nutritional supplement and allopathic treatment on offer. Healing, he suggests, is not a scientific algorithm, but a mysterious amalgamation of many elements. He remained open and curious, which is surely a directive, not just for facing illness, but all of life.

In the spirit of Nepo's openness and in case miracles also work by proxy, a few months after my mother's diagnosis, I made an appointment with an energetic practitioner.

Through a guided visualisation, I pictured my mother as a young woman on a beach, joyous, holidaying, the load of life's burdens, elsewhere, cradled in the moment by the sand beneath her feet and the endless sky above. In a bubble of light, she was unlatched to fear, and everything she loved was near and what was far, was loneliness and loss.

I'll never know if that ritual made any difference to my mother, energetically or otherwise. But it shifted my relationship with her illness to a new phase. There is a beautiful word for the stage between successive moults of insects like butterflies— 'instar.' That's what this ceremony of change felt like—it stripped me of the tight skin of despair that had cinched me for months.

I didn't tell my mother about it when we spoke. She would have found the whole thing ridiculous, not to mention a waste of money. Instead, I told her I'd had a beautiful dream of us at the beach together—like when I was little and she held my hand while we looked for shells.

'It was a very happy dream.'

'Nice to hear that,' she replied.

At the beach, I sometimes bump into an artist who makes protest art about climate change and ocean pollution from litter washed up by the ocean. She once told me that amongst the garbage, she occasionally comes across letters in bottles, written mostly by young women, desperate to lose weight, meet the right guy, love their bodies, have a child or give up smoking, alcohol or drugs.

Days later, from the cliff beyond the Bali memorial, I tossed a bottle with the message 'Please heal my mother' into the graciousness of the wild ocean.

While Emma was in France on a holiday, celebrating that she was finally seven weeks pregnant after years of infertility, a deep-vein thrombosis killed her. She was thirty-five. It took weeks before her body could be flown back to Australia.

I often think back to that day at the sushi train and wish I hadn't dismissed her premonition as fear. Perhaps intuition is fear's more grounded next-of-kin, and the job of spiritual growth is to learn to discern more carefully between old hauntings, echoes from the past we can learn to tune out of, and the ones that are trying to wake us into attention before it's too late.

Out in the open water, I often called Emma's name into the wind, asking her to watch over my mother, as she did when she held the hand of that dying girl who'd been hit by a bus.

Too often I have made the error of presuming I know the answer to other people's problems. It's a hubris, likely a throwback from parenting small children and a misguided saviour complex. I understand now that we must let others struggle and flail, even when we are convinced there is a life vest right under their seat.

The Buddhist teacher Jack Kornfield tells the story that after he discovered Buddhism, he was eager to share the joy of his enlightenment with his family, but they were not interested. He asked his teacher how he could impart some of his spiritual wisdom to them when all they wanted was to drink beer and watch football. How could he show them the light? His teacher answered, 'When you are with them, drink beer and watch football.'

As I flick through the movie options on the flight, I realise this is going to be my challenge when I land—to find the equivalent of beer and football with my mother.

During the Holocaust, when the Nazis were exterminating entire populations of Jews, homosexuals, communists and gypsies, most people did everything possible to save themselves and their families. But there were some, like Irène Némirovsky, a Russian-born, French-language novelist and Dutch writer Etty Hillesum, who chose not to escape their destiny. Etty accepted her fate and wrote '… everyone who seeks to save himself must surely realise that if he does not go, another must take his place…'

Later, she expressed, 'I don't ever want to be what they call 'safe.' I want to be there… I want to understand what is happening and share my knowledge with as many as I can possibly reach.'

Their astounding courage challenged my thinking about the imperative of seeking our survival at all costs. Perhaps it is bitter salvation to survive, if those we love do not; for their deaths change what makes life worth living. Nowhere has this been more painfully documented than in Sonali Derinyagala's book *Wave*, her memoir of how she lost her two boys, husband and both her parents, in the tsunami on Boxing Day in Sri Lanka in 2004. The sole survivor of her family, she was on suicide watch for years.

Perhaps there are times when it is our calling to be part of, not spared from, a terrible moment.

For months I discussed the conundrum of when to go to South Africa with a friend.

'This is not the time to be thinking. Just go. You never regret a heart decision,' he said.

It never felt like the right time: South Africa was consumed by a third wave of Covid, flights were exorbitant, and it was impossible to get travel insurance for Covid.

He simply shrugged and said, 'You're overthinking it. Don't suffer your future.'

I postponed my trip, once, twice, three times.

Then on a day in lockdown in August 2021, I was swimming across the bay, when I felt something brush past me. Not the sting of a jimble, those ghostly clear bell-shaped jellyfish, nor a bobbing bluebottle, just as searingly vicious. It wasn't the icky gloop of a Salp, a harmless jellied blob that disrupts your rhythm and appetite for the water. It was more like a sound; if you'll indulge me, even a *voice*.

I stopped, treaded water, pushed my goggles up onto my cap and looked up into the dazzle of the dancing ripples.

Go now.

Now?

Yes, right now.

It is not for me to say how or if God speaks to anyone, if at all, but I confess that I once made Zed get off a plane headed for Tasmania while we were delayed on the runway because this same nudge told me it wasn't safe to fly. He was angry and embarrassed that our departure would delay the flight even longer as the airline located and removed our baggage, all of which I saw in the face of a man convinced his wife was having a nervous breakdown in public. But bless him, he accompanied me off the plane, perhaps to afford me the privacy of a panic attack without spectators. Ten minutes later, the remaining passengers disembarked at the instruction of the captain, because, well, there was, in fact, a technical problem with the plane.

'What the hell...? How did you know?' he asked, incredulous.

I don't know. But I've come to trust these messages. They've saved my life, more than once.

We might get clarity from a dream. Goosebumps. A voice we hear out in the open water.

Sometimes a decision claims you, like an African fish eagle swipes its prey, a soundless bolt from above.

I needed to get to South Africa as soon as possible. What was I waiting for?

Time with my mother was precious. What was here would still be here when I returned. What was there was leaving me. All the months of hesitancy, faltering and desperation fell away.

The poet Rilke wrote, 'Let everything happen to you, beauty and terror.' To be in between worlds is to suffer. When we choose a path, we surrender to this everything.

I turned and swam back to shore.

That was three days ago.

Now, the captain's voice breaks my reverie. 'Ladies and gentlemen, we've begun our descent into Johannesburg. Cabin crew, prepare the cabin for landing.'

PART 2
GOING UNDER

CHAPTER 7

'Who is it?' I hear her voice through the intercom.

'Me, it's me, Mom.' My voice is small as I stand at the gate to my childhood home, my finger on the buzzer, my heart a wild falcon in my chest.

The metal gate slides open, and the Uber drives up the long driveway.

And suddenly, there she is, my at-long-last mother at the front door, always the first to greet, like the daughter in *Beauty and the Beast*. Her hair has grown back from the chemo, wavy and curly. She looks wonderful in her stretched hand-knitted grey turtleneck jumper. I'm not sure what scars I imagined cancer would drag across her, but there are none I can see. To hug her close is all I've wanted for what now feels like forever, and I wrap her in my arms, kissing the top of her head, as I tower over her.

'You look good, mama,' I say through my tears.

'Don't say that,' she chides, as she ushers me inside.

My father toddles towards me, bent as a sickle. His spine has never recovered from when he broke his neck as a young man in a Judo class, and the impact of that accident has played itself out in his old age. Every step he takes is a disaster about to happen. He is gregarious and delighted and suddenly, there is so much talking and familiarity, and I am swirling in the long history that these walls hold.

We make tea and sit together in the loungeroom. My mother asks about the kids, keen on every detail of their lives. I relay what little there is to report. With such enormities before us, she talks about *Jane the Virgin*, a telenovela on Netflix, which she's loving, and chatters on about the characters as if they are real people. Dad complains that she still loves reruns of *Judge Judy*, and if he has to listen to the horrible voiceover on *Come Dine With Me*, he'll lose his mind. Why is it necessary to spoil a good show with that commentary? But it's all said in good spirits. He will watch whatever she wants. My mother's copy of *What Shall I Make?* is beside her on the couch underneath take-away menus and remote controls.

'Your mother often pages through it, it's her favourite book,' he says. I smile. It is well-thumbed.

My mother tells me that on weekends, when Nomusa, their fantastic new domestic helper, goes home and they are alone in the house, Dad comes down every morning to make the coffee. He gets up to demonstrate how he carries two cups of coffee up that treacherous, winding staircase. He places the mugs a few steps ahead, takes a step up and then moves the mugs up another step and so on. It's adorable and kind of ridiculous all at once, though it makes me certain they should not be left alone in this big house. I notice he's developed a new habit of kissing his finger and touching the mezuzah on every door as he enters and exits every room. God help us if he has become religious again. Nobody enjoyed it the first time around when he became orthodox for a few riling years in my teens. I guess we are all clinging to the tendrils of faith as we know it.

A few weeks ago, when we spoke, I suggested my mother watch *Fabulous Fungi* on Netflix. I told her, 'It's all about mushrooms,' hoping she'd think it was a cooking show. It was my way of easing her into receiving the bottles of Turkey Tail mushroom tablets I have brought with me. I wanted her to hear the evidence that they can stop cancerous cells growing, though I was sure she would dismiss it as claptrap. She reads the small print on the container before swallowing a couple. Her openness to taking them, that's new.

I say we are going to party and celebrate over the next three months, every opportunity we get. She gives me an exasperated look.

A few hours later, my sisters arrive and swamp me with hugs and gifts and exclamations of *I can't believe you're here*. I suck in the affection like oxygen. The surge of urgency in our moments together now compresses a rare intimacy as we sit together in our childhood home.

In the late afternoon, when I can feel the jetlag stalking me, I follow my mother out into the garden. At the pool, she bends down to remove the leaves from the filter. She is still the do-er around here, the one who keeps everything working.

After my father's near-death experience a few years ago, my sisters and I launched a campaign to get them to sell the house and move into a smaller ground-level townhouse. We'd paid for a professional declutterer to help sort out the stash of stuff accumulated over decades. My mother resisted this like we were extracting toenails. But I see now that this house they love, with its lovely big garden and pool, is where they have needed to be during this pandemic. It has protected them from the contractions beyond these walls. Here, they are happy. It is where their lives began.

It was the middle of 1967, and my parents were on the way to the movies, but took a detour to have a quick look at 60 The Braids Road, a double-storey house in the leafy suburb of Greenside. They were living in an apartment in the hippie village of Yeoville with Carolyn, who was two at the time, and me on the way. My grandparents had met them for the inspection. The owners turned out to be old patients of my grandfather, Jack, the doctor who started the MBBCh streak in our family.

The story goes that my heavily pregnant mother walked through the front door, turned, and whispered to my father, 'I love it.'

They signed a contract right there and even made it to their movie on time.

This is the home to which I was driven from the Lady Dudley hospital after I was born. It's where I have brought my children to visit every year after we immigrated to Australia. It's the only house I ever dream about: the winding stairwell, the large wooden chest for storing linen in the entrance hall, the six-windowed, three-fridged kitchen with its ugly brown cupboards and linoleum flooring, my father's large messy art studio, the shed next to the pool my friends and I once converted into our secret cubby house, the toolshed at the back filled with garden equipment, the patch outside the laundry where my nanny Violet planted her corn and spinach, the overhanging mulberry tree which fed many seasons of silkworms, the odd-shaped loungeroom with too many doors and an unused piano, and the dining room with its pink velvet chairs.

It is a central character in my life story, this old house. I don't know who I am without it.

Later in the afternoon, at Carolyn's place, I unpack, hang up my clothes and plug in my South African adaptor to charge my iPhone. Over the next three months, I will sleep in twenty different beds. I will live out of the boot of my mother's car into which all my belongings are packed. It is just as well that I don't know this, as I sit at the kitchen table with my sister, dipping biscuits in tea, trying to believe I am finally here.

Carolyn tells me that she recently berated Dad for eating too many bananas. They are high in potassium, and as he has only one kidney, it can cause heart problems.

'And you know what he did? He asked for another one,' she says, shaking her head. 'He is determined to die before mom.'

Later, when I relay this to Zed on the phone, he responds, 'We call that, bananacide.'

'What about a walk around the Dam, to get a bit of fresh air?' I suggest to my mother the next morning.

When we came with the kids for our annual visits and stayed with them in previous visits, she and I would slip out every morning for a walk around the Emmarentia Dam and through the Botanical Gardens. We had some of our best talks on those walks in the days when she was fit and strong.

She shakes her head. 'I need to wait to see the oncologist to see where I am, if I'm getting better or worse.'

'What difference will that make?' I ask.

'Let's wait to see where I am with my treatment,' she repeats.

This interaction sets the tone for the coming days.

Understanding that we are unlike our parents is one of our first betrayals. It is also the beginning of the most important psychic journey of our lives—individuation. I have been defining myself on a different continent for almost twenty years, and every time I return, it becomes apparent that my parents don't know the person I have become, and I don't know who they are anymore. All my life I have wanted my mother to be a different kind of person, a different kind of mother. As a little girl, I believed for a long time that she could not be my real mother, because a true mother would not get cross when her child wakes with nightmares and tell her to 'just go back to bed.'

I notice I am thinking that if it were me, I would not put my life on hold and postpone any opportunity for joy, while waiting to hear if my cancer was getting better or worse. A walk in the fresh air can only be good for her, surely? But I have barged in on a situation that is eight months old. I do not understand the rules here. I am the visitor, with my radical interference, disrupting her TV watching and routines with my outrageous suggestions.

Perhaps it's the ocean in me now, the wildness my open water swimming has stirred in me—my longing for more nature and silence, and less television and noise. I want to remind her that there is more than *Tipping Point* and *MasterChef*—there are birds and trees and sky too. There is the sun on your face, and the water between your toes, and the way the light stipples through the branches and changes as the day ages.

Over the next few days, as I do the shopping and other chores around the house, I feel an agitation and frustration building in me. I haven't come all this way only to help with day-to-day tasks. I want to extend the comfort of a true and deep conversation, something that might steer my mother away from suffering her future, to help her be a little less afraid of what lies ahead. She is still here, she still belongs with us for now, even though part of her has been pulled far out, like a rip can take you before you blink.

But she wants nothing of it, nothing of what I am offering. I feel useless, spare, even though I am right in front of her.

Laura, sitting next to me on the couch, says, 'How cute is it when mom uses emojis?'

I hold my mother's hands in mine in a task I know is solemn and vital. She has short thumbs, a genetic condition known as brachydactyly, which Carolyn has inherited. She likes bright coloured nail polish, blues, pinks and purples, an adorable adolescent characteristic. She has agreed to let me massage her hands to ease the tingling from the neuropathy caused by the chemo.

I squeeze a dollop of delicious melon-smelling hand cream from The Bodyshop into my palms and rub it into her upturned hands. I press my thumbs gently into the cups of these appendages, which have, over my lifetime, felt my forehead for a temperature, rubbed my back with after-sun lotion, smoothed my hair, wiped my tears, guided me across busy streets, knitted me dolls' clothes and blankets, and cooked thousands, maybe tens of thousands of meals. Her hands are a comforting firmness in mine, and I work the cream into them, attending to each finger, knuckle, the webbing between fingers and her wrists.

'Thank you,' she says, before I have finished. It's her way of saying, enough.

I leave the cream on the loungeroom table so I can do it every day. I offer to massage her feet too. I want every opportunity to touch her, to let her know I am right beside her, not across the ocean, a face on screen.

'We'll see,' she says.

CHAPTER 8

A few mornings after my arrival, I make a batch of egg mayonnaise sandwiches with mustard, capers, lettuce and pickles and pack them in a little bag. It is a lure to get my father into the passenger seat of the car. He doesn't want to leave the house, but I am having none of it. I tempt him as I used to with my kids when they were small. 'We'll get takeaway coffees. We'll drive to the Zoo Lake, sit on a bench and look at the ducks. It will be good for you.'

When we get there, he doesn't fancy a walk around the lake, so we just sit in the car and eat our sandwiches. We are finished way too quickly—we still have hours to pass while my mother is having her scan. The results will dictate what the next few months will look like. I feel optimistic—she looks well, she seems well, it's hard to believe she has cancer.

I tell him about Etty Hillesum. I wish I'd brought her diaries for my father to read.

We sit in silence for a while, and then he says, 'Take me home.'

Late in the afternoon, when my mother returns from the hospital, she goes straight to the kitchen and rustles up the most spectacular chilli con carne. I ask her what the secret is.

'The best olive oil, of course. Curry leaves and fresh coriander.'

When she talks about food or gets excited about eating, she is not sick; she is herself, the mother I know.

I take over thinking and planning what we're going to eat for lunch every day. I can see it weighs heavily on her. I don't want to usurp her role, just to relieve her. I'm trying to implement what I learned from the book I read before I came, *Dignity for those who are Dying*, which stressed how important it is to preserve a sick person's 'continuity of self,' that ineffable quality of life which embodies all our human needs of honour, respect and esteem. Even if she cannot cook, she still needs to be involved in decisions about what to shop for. Each day, I ask her for a shopping list, I shop, return and then I cook, while she supervises.

Some things my mother is strict about. She doesn't like to feel the cold. She likes to be comfortable. She doesn't like tasteless food, which she invariably insists needs more salt. And when she's had enough, she's had enough. She once announced at the end of a meal, 'It's time to fuck off now,' before herding everyone out the front door. You generally know where you stand with her.

I am standing at the stove frying the South African sausage, *boerewors*, for lunch when she comes into the kitchen. She stands and watches. She tells me I have burnt it. Even her complaints make me happy. She is still fussy about how her sausage is cooked. It still matters.

I ask if, over the coming weeks, she'll show me how to make her ruby grapefruit marmalade. Every year, she makes a batch, and my dad draws handwritten labels for the jars with the date. Her pantry is still stocked with jars from various years past, like wines in a cellar. She says she will, we'll find a time.

Since Covid, my South African family has not had a Friday night dinner together. It has always been an enduring ritual of connection and the centre of my mother's week. I suggest we host one this week. I tell my mother I will do all the work, all the cleaning up. She can still be in bed early. I'm thrilled when she agrees.

We discuss Friday night's menu. We talk about how we each make salsa.

'I use onions and chilli,' she says.

We agree that we'll make two batches for Friday night's Mexican to cater for the wussier palates. Though we both agree, what's salsa without chilli?

I propose going out for a family breakfast on my birthday in a few days' time. My mother shakes her head. She doesn't want to leave the house until she hears back from the oncologist about her scan.

'Mom, when last did I spend a birthday with you? This may be the last birthday I get to celebrate with you.'

'It may be the last birthday of yours in which I'm alive,' she replies.

'Isn't that even more of a reason to celebrate?' I persist.

Even as I speak it, I realise the word 'celebrate' doesn't mean what it used to.

'Do you want to take a bet you'll be alive for my next birthday?' I ask.

There is a long and strange pause. She picks up the remote, switches on the TV and starts scrolling for something to watch.

Suddenly, I feel suffocated. I need to get out; I cannot be stuck watching reruns of *Judge Judy*. I am failing so utterly at the Jack Kornfield test. I drive to a nursery in a nearby suburb, where I spend a fortune on pansies and rose quartz rocks. I return and spend the afternoon planting the flowers in the window boxes outside the loungeroom, to revive the garden with colour while my folks sit inside, in front of the TV watching one show after the other. Maybe if I plant things, my mother will feel life vibrating around her; maybe if I bring nature to her, there will be enough beauty to keep her here longer. From the garden, I hear the canned laughter and applause, and I try not to gouge the plants as I press them frantically into the soil.

The next day, I am at the shops with a long list of groceries my mother has written down for me. Her tastes are specific and require diligent attention. *White cheddar from Checkers. The small wine gums in the tubs at the Woolworths counter. Obscure brands of mustards at delis. The extra-virgin olive oil she loves.* It's as if she's sending me on a scavenger hunt, testing my patience and fortitude. She's entrusted me with her credit card to pay for them.

While I'm walking the aisles, scouring the shelves for the olive oil she wants, a man approaches me holding a plastic bag with bread rolls. 'Mam, will you buy these for me please?' I am pierced by tears. Hunger in this country is on every street corner. It is in the face of every person you pass.

'Sure,' I swallow. 'Is there anything else you need?' He nods and heads off.

He returns, laden. He deposits two bags of newborn nappies and three tubs of baby formula on the counter. I pay for it all.

I cry all the way back to the house and arrive with mascara running down my cheeks. My father says I am crying to release all the emotion of the past week. Maybe that's true, but I am no longer emotionally fit for this country. My South African muscles have slackened. I need to toughen up.

When I tell my sisters about this encounter, they both laugh. I've been conned. It's a well-known sting. Privileged white woman approached by a 'beggar' in store to help with a loaf of bread, who then upsells her to expensive products he can take back to the township to sell. Oh well, does it matter? Babies somewhere will benefit from those nappies and baby food.

After these first few days, I am trying too hard. I have brought my cheerleading game, and my rambunctiousness and high energy are exhausting, not only for my parents but for me. With all my effort to shoo the negativity away, I'm overdoing the pompoms and high kicks. After twenty years in Australia, I'm an alien species landed on Planet Family, trying to remember how to speak their language.

Every day I swim in the freezing pool, a spectacle that entices my parents into the garden more often than they'd otherwise venture, if only to tell me I am crazy to get into such cold water. 'Oh Joanne,' my mother sighs. 'What will you do next?'

Each afternoon, I massage her hands.

I think she is glad I am here, but it's hard to tell. Perhaps it is too much of an omen of what her prognosis means that I have made such an effort. At times, she is engaged when we talk about food, my kids, and whatever's on TV. But mostly, she is distant, deep inside herself.

I pray the scan gives us good news, a tiny reprieve so she can have a few more months on a treatment that doesn't overwhelm her with punishing side effects. But whatever the coming days bring, I am here with her to face whatever we have to face. We will meet it all, together.

I spend the afternoon with her, chopping vegetables and preparing for the first Shabbat our family will have together this whole year—a Mexican feast to celebrate my brother-in-law's birthday. We make salsa and guacamole, refried beans and beef mince.

My mother frets about what time the mince should be warmed up, how hot the oven needs to be, how and when we should serve what. I accede to all her decisions and let her take charge. We make gorgeous pink gin and tonics with a fancy mandarin gin I bought for her. I slice oranges and strawberries for the glasses, so they glisten, bejewelled. We *le'chaim* over these orange beauties.

I come sit by her side and hold her hand. I tell her that no matter what the chemo markers show, we still have treatment options. None of my consolations reach her. Her lips are tight; her face pinched with creases of anxiety.

As much as we are all surrounding her, ultimately, people travel the terrifying road of terminal illness alone.

That evening, before dessert is served, my mother seems tired. I can see it is time for us to leave, so we all clear the table and pack the leftovers into Tupperware. She has no appetite for cake or even a taste of the fruit salad I made with gooseberries and blueberries the size of strawberries. I hug her goodnight. She seems faraway, stretched, out of reach.

Back at Carolyn's house, my sister pulls me aside, her face in a frown. She has access to all the pathology results and tells me that during dinner, she received an email with my mother's updated cancer markers. They have tripled. From 190 to over 650. It means the oral chemo isn't working. I feel a physical jolt.

Then, oh God, I realise that my mother knew—Carolyn had told her just before dessert. She told us in her frail voice when she said she was tired. My mama, so silent and so brave.

Carolyn and I lie on her bed, the quiet horror between us. We discuss whether we should tell Laura—we don't want to spoil her husband's birthday, perhaps it can wait until tomorrow.

I say, 'She needs to know now.' This is important.

So, we Facetime my little sister. I watch her face fall as we explain.

The three of us try to take it in. What it means. What lies ahead. Carolyn goes into doctor mode, explaining the results to us. *What it means. What it means.* We talk about how afraid both mom and dad are, they are like our children. I tell Carolyn she has become a mother to our mother. We must all look after her now.

Carolyn says she's afraid that when our parents die, I will have no reason to come back to South Africa to visit. I tell her, I will.

'Promise?' she asks tearfully.

'I promise.'

We are all thinking far ahead, beyond parents, even beyond husbands.

I lie awake into the gloomy hours, my thoughts tumbling and knocking around in my head. If all my mother has left is another year or eighteen months, shouldn't I stay with her until the end? Here, I can make a difference, share the load with my sisters and support my parents. Suddenly, my life in Sydney feels like a strange dream, beyond reach. Is it even real?

I've only been here a week.

'We're going to live our lives,' my dad says the next morning when I arrive at the house.

It's the first time he's drawn on all the philosophy and mysticism he claims have animated his life. My father likes to tell the story of how he met the Lubavitcher Rebbe Menachem Schneersen in Crown Heights decades ago, a great spiritual leader and mystic who apparently could see the past, present and future all at once. When he and my mother had '*yechidut*,' the privilege of a few minutes alone with him to receive a personal blessing, the Rebbe told him to 'finish his book,' long before my father ever contemplated writing one. Then, he turned to my mother and said, 'Attend to the healing of the spirit as much as to the body.' Prophetic words.

Today, my mother also seems calmer—perhaps simply knowing what is going on allows the psyche to settle. More than it just being a cancer marker, it is a marker of place, it positions her, she knows where she is—that's what she's been saying all this time, 'I just want to know where I am.'

Some of us are fixated on the numbers, test results, what the biology is showing, but there are other indicators of her wellness—her appetite, mood, how she looks and feels. We must also focus on these. They, too, are sources of health and strength. I remind her every day to take the Turkey Tail mushroom tablets, and bless her, she faithfully swallows them.

Meanwhile, I revel in being with my sisters. I go shopping with Carolyn for my birthday gift, we try on clothes, I walk to a café to get morning coffee for her, we lie on her bed or sit on the swing from our childhood in her garden sipping on pink gins and tonics.

Laura and I lie across her bed, rifling through her jewellery collection, swapping rings and laughing hysterically at something only the two of us find funny, remembering that we share the identical taste in music (once when I came to visit, we both had Robbie Williams' song 'Angels' as our ringtones). When we were growing up, we'd sit at the end of the table and tell stories just between us, in our sisterly world. My immigration broke her heart, she often tells me. Back then, I was too fixated on my end to consider the devastation we left in our wake.

Only now that I am here with them do I let myself feel how much I miss them. When we are all together, I am sistered. I am the glue between them. Something is restored. I am part of what makes this family whole. Here, I reawaken, like *Sleeping Beauty* to the sheer joy of being the middle sister. I am drenched with attention, reminded of how deeply and well they know me, my tastes in clothes, jewellery, food, music. They return stories from the past to me, and colour in the places and past we have traversed together.

When I am in Sydney, the threads that hold this unit together slacken, and when I am here, I am frayed from my children and Zed—the family that makes me mother and partner. I shuttle between these chambers of my heart and must numb the half I am far from, so that grief and loss do not pierce me ragged.

I am forever split, divided. I am always half somewhere and half nowhere. I can never just be whole in one place.

The next morning, I wake up early to get coffees for everyone. I want to bring my mother a cappuccino from her favourite coffee shop before she goes to see her doctor to discuss what's next.

As she's leaving with Carolyn, my father approaches to hug her in an anxious clutch, and she berates, 'Don't, just don't... be cool.' She reins him in.

While they're gone, I take my father for a long, slow walk around the block.

He tells me that last night, they were lying on the bed, and she'd said, 'I love my life—I love my children, I love watching TV, I love cooking and eating, and I love my house.' It pierces me, this enumeration of all the things she is going to miss.

My father cries freely. I sometimes think losing his mother young punctured an unfixable hole in the bucket of his heart. Unlike my mother, he never has any trouble expressing his feelings. I tell him that he's part of the life she loves. This is her way of telling him that she loves him.

We wait nervously for news, and finally Carolyn sends the voice memo from the session with the doctor who begins with, 'It's not good news.' No surgery is possible because the cancer has spread, but thankfully not to her liver or lungs. The doctor says she's putting her on six months of chemo, with extreme side effects, including nausea and tingling in her fingers and even possible high-frequency hearing loss. It all sounds horrible.

The toughest is hearing her ask in a voice so shaky, my heart hurts to hear it, 'So I'll have six months?' and the doctor says, 'You'll have more than six months.'

I hear my mother ask if she can up the dosage of her anti-depressant.

Back home, I ask her if she wants to try visualising her cancer disappearing as one of Dad's friends did when he had cancer—he's now in remission—and she says, 'I wish I believed all that stuff.' I swallow down all my longing for her to just try it, instead of finding reasons to say no. I don't tell her about Mark Nepo. I know it would make no difference.

I jump into the pool where the icy August water burns me, and I force myself to stay in until the cold is deep inside my aching muscles. The treatment she is agreeing to sounds more like abuse than a cure. When do 'side-effects' take over, like a metastasising cancer, and become 'effects'? What kind of a life will it be as the poisons flood her system?

I spend the afternoon gardening, planting succulents in pots outside. I don't know what else to do with myself. Inside, my mother watches cooking and game shows, where people are congratulated for what they've done with mystery box ingredients and summarily and randomly eliminated. *Drink beer and watch footy*, I remind myself. This is *her* life, and more importantly, her dying time, and she must do it exactly as she wants to. Even if it means more TV, more antidepressants.

Our time is coming to an end, one way or the other. As if I didn't know that, as if I imagined somehow, it was not the case. Alone in the garden, my tears fall freely. This disease is marching on, an unstoppable force of nature. I want it to cease, halt, just slow down so my kids can see their Nana just one more time, so I can make good my promise on her 80th birthday, that I would bring them back. Now the first line of Galway Kinnell's poem 'Prayer', comes to me, and I repeat it over and over like a mantra, 'Whatever happens…' I must be careful not to want things to be different from how they are. I must want only what is. Whatever it is.

As I look through the window at my parents sitting side-by-side in the loungeroom, holding hands, I long to really be with her and my father, as we face this strange wrapping up, this foreclosure on her body, and presence in our lives. We must be brave for her who is the bravest of all. We cannot let her see how her suffering grips us, how we each wish we could take on some of it for her, so she doesn't have to do it all alone.

In my gardening frenzy, I pull out all the weeds. I find what looks like a patch of weeds growing from the round brick structure near the front door, and I try to yank them out, but the roots are deep. I intend to plant succulents in their place.

Later, when my mother comes outside and sees the desecrated patch, she is furious. 'Why did you pull out my flowers? They were about to bloom.'

'I thought they were weeds.'

My mother shakes her head and my heart falls.

CHAPTER 9

We are sitting outside in the garden of a little restaurant under umbrellas for my birthday breakfast. No-one is in the mood for celebrating, least of all me. I can't quite work out why I insisted. Maybe it's just to see my mother as I have always known her—paging through a menu and planning her gastronomic pleasure. She always recites dishes out loud, sounding them out, the way I read poems: *I wonder how they do their shakshuka; the haloumi stack sounds nice; maybe with a side of mushrooms…*

She orders a toasted tuna sandwich, and I pray it's the best bloody tuna sandwich ever toasted. I encourage her to have another cappuccino. '*Do you want a third?*' We wrap it all up quickly because she wants to get home.

On the way home in the car, I ask my dad where my birthday card is. He says he isn't in the mood to make one.

'Dad, sometimes we just have to rally and do things even if we don't feel like it.'

When we get back to the house, he trundles upstairs resignedly to make me a card. I'm not proud of how desperate and manipulative I am being. But I also have needs.

His absence gives my mother and me some rare time alone together downstairs.

Without my father hovering, she speaks to me.

'I've doubled my dose of antidepressants.'

I hear something beneath those words, a cue.

My mother is trying to tell me something. I come to sit beside her, and I take her hands in mine.

'Are you depressed?' I ask.

'I'm anxious and panicky, and I don't like that feeling.'

'Panicky about the chemo and side effects?'

'About the whole diagnosis.'

I take my time. I choose my words. I speak carefully and slowly. I don't want to scare her off, just as she has ventured like a deer into the clearing.

'Mom, it's normal to be afraid of death,' I pause, '… but maybe it's not as scary as we think it is. Are you afraid of leaving Dad?'

'Yes.' I notice she is trembling. 'And I always thought I'd live to a ripe old age.'

'You still might,' I say. 'You never know how you might react to the chemo, let's wait and see.'

'I have a year or two at most,' she says.

This here is the truth we both know. It has been said. The medical reality. I close my eyes and ask for this not to be so. If this is how it is, how do we make space for miracles?

I massage her hands and her tight shoulders. Every time I touch her, I am grounded, skin to skin. I shudder at what her poor body has to go through with the chemo. Ever since I was a teenager, I have loomed large over her, beanstalked with my father's genes. Despite her little stature, I have always thought of her as a lioness. She is formidable and has already withstood so much. She says she is ready to take on whatever the chemo brings. She is adamant that she wants to live.

'I have to,' she says emphatically. 'It's just a bit of nausea.'

My father's card is so beautiful that it makes me cry. He's drawn me as 'God's gardener,' planting light in the shadows.

Later that day, we're sitting in the loungeroom drinking tea, and my mother says that Laura sent her a message to say that she is her best friend.

'It's overwhelming to hear that,' she confesses. 'But we have become very close.'

Before Covid, she tells me, they'd often meet at the gym for water aerobics. Laura also comes over a few times a week to help her do their accounts online, and they sit together at the computer in my old room.

Perhaps my mother battles to think of herself as anyone's 'best friend,' because of her struggles through a friendless childhood. But somehow, this is different, a closeness adulthood has gifted them both, and I am warmed to tears by this confession. My heart lurches as I think of my children—they are, without doubt, the two people I would choose to spend time with before anyone else. I squeeze the ache inside me until it is numb. Right now, I have no space for missing anyone else but my disappearing mother.

That night, my sisters and niece Jenna take me out to a Greek restaurant for dinner. We try and try and try to celebrate. Waiters bring a dessert with a sparkler and stand around singing Happy Birthday. But devastation festers underneath, I can feel sorrow's harmonising score.

That night, Dad has a panic attack. He retches and vomits. When I hear this news, I strain for compassion and wish I could stifle my judgment that my mother has selflessly served all his needs as an artist all his life, and yet he can't be strong for her when she needs him. She's being pumped with chemo. She's facing this horrible prognosis. And she must worry about *him* falling apart. *Get a grip, Dad*, I want to shout.

My mother declares she's going to make lamb curry for Friday night—she wants to eat as much spicy food as she can, while she can, before the chemo takes her appetite. Something about this holds a desperation, a dreadful momentum.

After two weeks in South Africa, I'm giddy with the freedom of being in a country without strict Covid regulations. When I speak to Zed every day, I am loaded with guilty relief that I am out of the vice of the lockdown that is bolting life down in Sydney and Melbourne. People are literally trapped in their homes indefinitely. I feel reckless. I want to splurge and make the most of my liberty. I drive to the Linden Public Pool, just to be a person among people, though I find myself one of two swimmers there. Still, I am out and about.

For Jewish New Year, my mother needs 'ingredients,' she tells me. She doesn't want to send me to the shops, even with a list, because I won't know exactly what she needs and I'll get the wrong thing. I offer to be her chauffeur. Our first stop is her favourite place, the Spice Shop, a cramped emporium of shelves in an Indian market. I watch as she moves amongst the aisles, all masked up, clutching a basket, thinking about flavours and delicious things to cook. Here, she is in her element, with fresh cumin, curry leaves and rich cardamom in our nostrils. Her delight is simple as she fills her basket and pays for more spices than she needs.

Next, I drive her to the Fish Shop where she scours the passages, selecting the various fish for the dishes she's planning. She asks for this to be skinned, that to be filleted, and the other to be chopped. I'm aware of a strange, premature nostalgia, like I'm looking back on this moment already. I wonder if this is how climatologists view every passing season, each event that passes, wondering, 'Is this the last?'

Outside a woman is selling freshly fried samosas. I buy thirty, an outrageous binge, as if this is the very last samosa hurrah—ten chicken, ten lamb, ten cheese and corn, and we eat them nonstop on the way home, passing them between us. She chides me for overspending, overindulging, but only half-heartedly. This is how we play when she comes to Sydney as the visiting grandmother. My mother knows how to make a festival of eating. Everything in abundance, everything must be tasted. She is a greedy, clumsy child, filling her pockets and her cheeks with the pleasure of the next bite.

Back home, she sets about making gefilte fish. The house is permeated with the fishiest smell, and yet, those fish balls, when ready, are exquisitely light and appetising.

I give my father a journal and suggest he keeps a gratitude journal to jot down three things he's grateful for every day. He says, 'I probably won't use it.'

Time continues to spill away, but after a fortnight, I have fallen into a semi-routine. I visit my parents every day, spend lunch and the afternoon with them. I water the garden. We have a gin and tonic. We eat. We watch TV. My father rambles into one of his endless monologues, as if the talking can stall the onslaught of the darkness.

My sisters tell me they are glad I am here, picking up the slack around the day-to-day tasks and rallying for Shabbat dinners, each one precious, an endangered ritual. It is good to be useful, to know my presence here is making a difference.

Laura and I spend an afternoon planting a beautiful succulent garden out the back by Nomusa's room from cuttings we collected on one of our walks. It thrills me every time, breaking off a cutting, replanting it, and watching it bloom into a whole new plant. Small miracles.

One afternoon, I am alone in the garden. Everything is overrun and choked. I tear down dead branches from the prunus tree. I want to pull out all the overgrown and dead plants and replace them with succulents, colours, and beds of roses, my mother's favourites.

I turn and face the house, and all of a sudden, it's as if I'm looking at it from very far away. We know one another's every idiosyncrasy, nook and cranny, even as we both wear the beatings of time and cannot hide the failures of upkeep. Whenever I'm here, I revisit each corner of this building, where memories curl around corners, and olden times nestle in nooks.

This is the home that nursed my wounds—from the torn tendons in my hand as a toddler, to the heartbreaks of my first boyfriend's betrayal. In this garden, I celebrated parties, practised my netball shot and got stung by a bee on my buttocks. In this driveway, I was consumed by passion on the bonnet of a car and watched a man drive away, not knowing if I'd ever see him again. Here I have been loved on purpose, too much and too little, by inches and by miles. Here is where my life started. On this sacred ground, I uttered my first words, penned my first poems. Legends of my imagined future were hatched in these rooms; disappointments found me too.

This is the home I first left at fifteen for a three-month sojourn overseas and left again in my early twenties to study in America. I have been returning to these walls every year with a suitcase full of Australian gifts, lugging it up the steep stairwell I used to tear up and down a hundred times a day as a girl. It is the home I dream of when I am ill, and it's the place I pine for when I am lost. This architecture holds all my previous incarnations, and it is these rooms I long for when I am suffocated by homesickness.

My past is all around, still breathing in these walls. It reaches for me. 'Don't forget me,' it always whispers as my heart unspools. Here I am both storied and historied; understood and misunderstood, because as much as we belong to the past, we also outgrow it.

I can see through these walls, as I do in my dreams. This house is a nostalgic hologram inside me. The kitchen is just the same as I left it when I moved out as a young woman starting my own life. The empty glass jars on the windowsill haven't moved in thirty years. The adult in me wants to sweep them into the bin. The sputtering shower in the bathroom needs an upgrade. The child in me wants this place to never change. For nothing to be 'fixed.' How things were broken and remain so, is built into the scaffolding of my own inherited shattering. For many years, I was comforted by all this chaos-going-nowhere. But now it feels portentous.

For two decades I have managed my nostalgia, like an addiction, not letting it get its fingers around my throat. *No thanks, I don't do Longing-Things-Were-Different anymore. I've done my time. I've made my peace.* There is life in Australia, made of a different sky and earth and even love. Exile is a life built on grief. You can grow calluses in your softest places, eventually.

Like all disciplines of return—prayer, meditation, writing, intimacy—coming back to this place is an ongoing act of devotion.

But this time, it's different. Even the house knows it.

Now I am a refugee, here to collect a self I left behind in childhood. She is somewhere here in the mess. Part of what I'm doing here is searching for her.

I wish I had a way to ease my mother's fear, for that would be how I would tame my own. I would go back to that dark room where a little girl wakes from a nightmare and tell her that fear is not a way to know yourself or the world. I would wrap her in my arms and promise her, 'There will come a time when you will swim far beyond the breakers. People will ask, amazed, 'Are you not afraid of sharks?' And though you will be careful, you'll also be brave enough to swim out far. I promise you, my darling, someday, that will be you.'

CHAPTER 10

Several years back, as part of my mission to conquer my fears and get to the source of my deep-rooted anxieties, I found myself in a room with a transpersonal Jungian psychotherapist. Her specialty was sand play, a non-verbal symbolic technique that accesses the unconscious mind to make our inner worlds visible. I needed something that bypassed language and came through the back door of thought. She'd invited me to choose an object to symbolise my childhood from shelves choc-a-bloc with thousands of miniature figurines.

I'd reached for her instinctively — the green and black witch, her curled finger pointed, reminiscent of the uninvited witch in Sleeping Beauty who bursts into the christening and damns the baby princess.

'Why the wicked witch?' she had asked me.

'It felt like my childhood was cursed,' I said. I did not know until then that this is how it was for me.

'Cursed how?' she asked.

'There was just so much sadness. But I don't understand…I had a happy childhood…'

'These emotions don't necessarily belong to us; they might be wedged in our parents. Sometimes these stories don't even belong to them,' she said kindly, 'but we unwittingly carry what we don't understand.'

I first learned about family systems theory from one of the psychologists I'd interviewed when I was writing a book on raising teenagers when my kids were that age. She'd explained that a pathology in one family member does not pop up out of context but is rather a product of the entire family system. Each of us bursts forth from the soil not only of our parents, but our extended families. We are a compost of stories, traumas and ideologies built up over generations. I went on to read every book by James Hollis, a Jungian psychoanalyst and author who helped me understand that our 'hauntings' include the unlived lives of our parents and even grandparents. It seems the closest we can come to defusing our paranoias and exposing our blind spots is by unpacking the narratives we've been lugging around, like a drug mule who has no idea what's in the luggage they've been hoodwinked into shlepping across borders.

We have to travel back down the crazy river of our family's collective grief, to find what has poisoned our amniotic well. The benefit of this journey is that we can intentionally choose to let go of what we're unconsciously carrying.

I had grown up in a middle-class Jewish family in South Africa in the 1960s, raised by decent, good and generous parents. They both worked hard to send us to private schools. We lived in a beautiful big house with a pool and a garden. It had all the elements of a golden start to life.

But the climate in our home was taut and tense and filled with my father's explosive temper and my mother's quiet, coiled anxiety. Our nanny, Violet Matlapeng, like most domestic workers, was separated from her family and lived in a small backroom behind the kitchen. She travelled home twice a year, for Easter and Christmas; and occasionally, over school holidays, her two daughters came to stay for a few weeks. From the earliest age, I was pained by the injustice of this normalised arrangement and cried hysterically when Violet's baby girl Refilwe was sent back to live with her grandmother when she was a few months old. I resented my parents for their collusion with this unfairness. The politics of Apartheid's state-sponsored violence, inequality and racism played out not only beyond our high walls but within our home.

A child should never be kept from their mother, this, I knew.

Distance from.
Can't get to.
Out of reach.
Wherever I looked in my family's story, this pattern popped up.

When my father was just a little boy of eight, his mother Chaya, suffered a massive heart attack. From then on, he once told me, he knew she was going to die, and he'd cry himself to sleep every night. His parents were Ashkenazi Jewish immigrants who had escaped Eastern Europe in the 1920s and arrived in South Africa, leaving behind their extended family. Chaya's cardiac trouble began after her parents, sister, brothers and nephew were murdered in Naryshkin Park in the village of Zagare in Lithuania in 1941 and buried in a mass grave. We now have a name for stress that attacks the heart muscle—Takotsubo cardiomyopathy.

She never recovered. Her health deteriorated, and she died when my father was thirteen.

Three years later, in an act of misconstrued charity, my grandfather married my father's Hebrew teacher, Fanya, a Holocaust survivor whose husband and son had been murdered in the concentration camps.

Fanya tried to insist my father call her 'mother.' He refused, not even to placate a survivor of Dachau. He couldn't wait to escape the cheerlessness of his family home, and at twenty-two, he fled into the arms of the most beautiful woman he had ever seen, my mother, Dorrine, a medical student.

My mother was the long-awaited daughter of my nervous, timid Granny Bee, glamorous as a film star whose mother Doris died at thirty-six of tuberculosis when my granny was sixteen and then, in her words, 'my world fell apart.' She was forced to leave school, and soon after, her father remarried her mother's sister.

If one can make any observation about the men in my family, it's that they have made some truly clueless second-marriage decisions.

My charming and handsome grandfather, Jack, a lawyer at the time, pursued and pressured my granny to marry him. On their honeymoon, she contracted tuberculosis and nearly died. When she recovered, he was inspired to abandon law and study medicine. After she struggled for eight years to have a baby, my mother finally arrived. As a little girl, my mother nagged for a sibling, but my granny had miscarriage after miscarriage, and after losing a baby when she was six months pregnant, she finally gave up trying. 'It was a boy, I believe,' she once said when I pressed her for details.

'Did you have any therapy? Anyone to talk to?' I'd inquired when I'd once interviewed her about her history.

'Oh no, my darling, in those days you just got on with it,' she chirruped.

I will never know the secrets of my mother's bleak childhood as she resigned herself to being an only child. She once intimated that she'd witnessed some grim dynamics in that cold, sad home where everyone was grieving and no-one spoke. But lonely people find ways to belong to the world. My mother lived in her imagination. She drew happy little mouse families celebrating weddings and holidays together.

My granny often said of her, 'She was as good as gold' and 'never gave us a second of worry,' even though she had a 'nervous cough' all her life. My shy and anxious mother had few friends through school. She studied hard to get good grades. If she came back with 95 per cent on a test, her father would ask, 'What happened to the other five per cent?' She begged him to be allowed to have a nose job, but he refused, one of his few decent acts of parenting. My mother wanted to study occupational therapy, but he vetoed it. 'If you're going into medicine, you'd better be the one giving the orders. Become a doctor.'

She didn't want to be anything as serious as a doctor. She was a romantic. She drew, painted and crafted paper dolls with hundreds of exquisite outfits. She knitted and crocheted entire wardrobes for her dolls. But mostly, she was a dutiful daughter.

Medical school was hell, 'the worst years of my life,' she once told me. Apart from the strain of the mind-distorting workload, as one of a handful of female medical students, she was bullied by professors, doctors and other male students who mocked and berated her for taking a spot away from a man, a 'real doctor.' Women were, after all, only interested in having children.

The first time my mother met my father, she told me, she couldn't bear him. He was a rowdy show-off, too Jewish, unsophisticated. But warmth. Oh, he had warmth. And humour.

'Why is everyone shouting at each other?' she asked, horrified after a meal with his boisterous family.

'Shouting? We're just talking,' he said.

After the bleak tiptoeing silences she came from, talking was too loud. My father filled the tracts of her loneliness with laughter. She too couldn't wait to flee her home.

They were married at twenty-two. My mother fell pregnant three years later with my sister Carolyn while she was doing her internship at the Fever Hospital, where she picked up a viral infection that caused Carolyn's hearing loss. The taunts had been spot-on. She had just wanted babies.

'August 1967 was the darkest time of my life,' my father once told me.

'What do you mean, Dad? That's when I was born.'

'Yes, and that is when the doctors told us Carolyn was brain-damaged.'

I was born into an emotional shitstorm. My mother was a few weeks away from giving birth to me when doctors misdiagnosed my sister's delayed developmental milestones as minimal brain damage. My father describes the dark curtain that fell over them. My mother, desperate to find out if I was 'normal,' insisted on being induced weeks before my due date. So, I arrived early, not on my own schedule, but to assuage my mother's fear. It was, it turns out, a lot to live up to and into.

Carolyn was properly diagnosed as hard-of-hearing weeks after my accelerated arrival. But my mother's milk dried up from the stress, and I was bottle-fed, mostly by my nanny Violet. From then on, ours was a family deeply preoccupied with a child with special needs. When I learned to speak, at around nine months, I was the only one who could understand my big sister before speech therapy guided her to speak clearly. So, I acted as Carolyn's interpreter.

Then, as a toddler of eighteen months, I was left unsupervised in the backyard, with a glass milk bottle and a boisterous puppy, resulting in a freak accident where the tendons in my left hand were shredded, and I nearly lost my middle finger. I needed numerous operations to fix my hand; combined with surgeries to remove tonsils and drain my sinuses, I was in and out of hospital over quite a few years.

Here is where I must have subconsciously figured out my place in a family with a special-needs child. I got the most love and attention when I was sick. There was nothing like a raging temperature or inflamed tonsils to thrust me into the spotlight of my mother's affection, bringing her close to hold her palm against my forehead, spoon medicine into my mouth, rub Vicks into my chest, make chicken soup and check to see I'd eaten it. Most importantly, she would worry about me. When I was well, I'd fade into invisibility. Being an invalid was dependably validating.

My mother didn't want to treat her own children, so she'd often call Dr Stan, a gentle GP who made home visits. I still remember his kind face, the way he'd try to warm the stethoscope before sliding up the back of my nightie onto my back to listen to my heart; the sturdy press of his fingers against my wrist, the sweet white syrup of the Amoxil, which had to be kept in the fridge. As the bottle emptied, I readied myself for wellness and the relegation back to self-sufficiency, planning my next illness.

But with all my health issues, I developed a paralysing fear of hospitals and medical procedures. To this day, all it takes is a whiff of disinfectant or the squeak of the wheels of a hospital bed to thrust me back into the vast terror of those buildings in which people often go to die.

My father once told me that before his mother died, he was allowed to visit her in hospital. But when he saw her lying in bed through the porthole of glass in the hospital door, his worst fears bearing down, he became hysterical. His cousin Sike hit him across the face to 'calm him down.' The last time he ever saw his mother, she took his hands in hers and stated, 'My son, it's no good.'

Did she mean her prognosis or the whole 'it' of life? How could he tell?

Eventually, my father turned to God, and who can blame him? When I was a teenager, he fell in with a miracle-promising-Messiah-invoking crowd of Jews and became fanatically religious, unwillingly roping our family into his 'can't do this or that' version of orthodoxy. My father prayed daily, sometimes with phylacteries and often to the point of weeping as if he were incanting against an inevitable fate. How terrifying it must have been to be the father to three daughters, one with a profound hearing loss, carrying the curse of 'it's no good,' passed down from his mother in the last moments of her life. How desperately he must have needed it to be otherwise.

I have often thought about my Bobba's words, and whether it was not so much a curse as a premonition, like Emma's, that the end was coming.

CHAPTER 11

I am standing beside my mother in her kitchen, trying to be helpful. I hover, not wanting to get in her way. Despite all the ways she has hidden how life has hurt her, at the stove, she is always full of pleasure, and it is hard to take my eyes off her.

Ever since I was small, I have watched her in an apron, talk radio on, pots sizzling, peeled onions lined up, waiting their turn as she sprinkles, stirs and seasons whatever is cooking, always in the best olive oil. In the mulberry summer, when our tree bore fruit, her jam would burp a sticky burgundy storm. On Passover, the dumplings would churn and chatter in the chicken soup.

My mother makes food the way some people sing; it rolls out of her, a generous, boundless creativity. She cooks to keep the peace, quieten the thunder, soften bruises, cool the African heat, heat the winter Highveld chill and keep us together. She has never thought of herself as an artist—that word is somehow too grand for her to stand it—but she can concoct a feast from the simplest of ingredients: an egg, potato, tin of pilchards, bouquet of radishes or leftover chicken carcass. In her quietness, a shyness often misunderstood as aloofness, she knows how to unlock the hidden masterpiece modesty conceals, the way Michelangelo saw the angel in the marble.

Now, even as the illness and its curative poisons course through her, she is making *kneidlach*, chopped herring, gefilte fish, mock crayfish. She spends the whole day cooking. One brother-in-law doesn't eat chicken; another doesn't like garlic or chilli. No problem, she caters for all these preferences as if they really matter at a time like this. Because, God forbid, anyone should leave hungry.

Her energy begins to flag before everyone starts to arrive for Rosh Hashana, Jewish New Year. I know we won't have long before she chases everyone away.

Dinner is a one-hour affair. My sisters congratulate me for pulling it off. Without my insistence, it wouldn't have happened.

But I am weaving the last strands of life, frantically spinning memories for the threadbare days ahead.

We're eating the many leftover fish dishes from Rosh Hashana for lunch when my mother says, 'Dad's hearing isn't so good.'

'What's wrong with the herring? I think it's delicious,' my father retorts.

We laugh, but are jokes about people mishearing funny?

We'd never laugh at Carolyn mishearing something. But these are desperate times.

Dad wanders from his chair to the loo and back again, with a kiss-the-mezuzah tic. I watch it all, as if from far away—we are here, together, but I feel remote. I try to pull myself back into the present, into my body, but even my skin feels odd. There's a puncture somewhere, and I feel the leak.

My niece Jenna is a fully grown woman. We have spent so little time together in our lives – what I know of her is mostly from updates my mother shares. But she is my sister's daughter, and as such, like my own child. My love for her is irrational and enormous.

She takes time away from her studies to have breakfast with me at a nearby café. On our walk, we both spot it on the ground—a butterfly that seems to be dead. She lifts it carefully in her palm, and when we reach the café, we mix a restoring cocktail of water and sugar in a saucer. She places the butterfly in it, and we watch as it slowly sips and revives. Our eyes meet tearfully. Maybe this is a good sign. Please, let it be a sign.

That night Carolyn organises a barbeque in her garden, to 'make the most of mom's appetite before the chemo starts.' While her husband gets a fire going, we sit around waiting for the coals to be ready, sipping drinks. My mother is even more impatient and irritable than usual — *she's hungry, she's cold, when will it be ready? She needs a blanket for her knees. What's taking so long*? The sausage on the grid over the fire still needs time, so I march the tray of lambchops indoors and fry them up in a pan on the stove to hurry things along. My mother just wants to eat and go home. We run around her, appeasing each request and unspoken demand. It's a relief when the *boerewors* is cooked perfectly—juicy just the way she likes it. Around the table in my sister's lovely garden, as the evening sidles in, we are a strained party in this frantic grasping at a ritual that, it turns out, cannot be hurried. There is nothing fun or enjoyable about a meal on death row, even of your favourite food. We go through the motions, and it is a colourless effort that leaves us bewildered.

The months of being my mother's sole support person are starting to wear Carolyn down. Her body is aching and tender. She's irritable and snappy and desperately needs time-out. She and her husband plan a couple of days away in the bush.

'Why don't you come with us?' Carolyn offers.

I am tempted. It's been decades since I last saw wildlife, the African terrestrial equivalent of my encounters in the open water, and my heart silently pleads for the sweet gift of a zebra, giraffe or elephant. But my needs right now are irrelevant.

'I don't think I can,' I say. 'Mom is starting her next round of chemo, and it's my turn to step up.'

Carolyn is limp with gratitude. She just needs a few days to herself, but I can tell she feels guilty prioritising her own needs. I am anxious about the timing of it, but surely, I can replace her for a few days. How hard can it be? I can drive. I can cook. I can shop.

When I tell mom I will take over all of Carolyn's duties while she's away, she can't hide her disappointment. I am not a doctor; I am not the one who has held her hand throughout this journey. I reassure her that I will try my best to be a good replacement.

She shrugs. I will have to do.

While my mother spends the day in chemo, Nomusa and I work alongside each other in the kitchen. I am making my mother's chicken soup from her recipe, for when she gets home. I put it on a slow simmer, with fresh turmeric, ginger and garlic, so that all the goodness will gently draw out. As the day grows longer, and the treatment is not yet over, my father's anxiety winds to a crescendo.

'I'm so afraid,' he keeps repeating. His face is crushed at the thought of what she's going through. I know he would trade places with her if he could.

'I wish we could go at the same time,' he says, like parents of his friend Russell who were killed simultaneously in a car accident.

'Unless it was a suicide pact, Dad, it would be ugly.'

'This is worse,' he sighs.

In the late afternoon, my mother sends a WhatsApp message in the family group 'Did Nomusa make chicken curry?'

'Yes,' I reply.

'How is it?'

I chuckle. Even while she's hooked up for four hours first on saline and then on the chemo, she is still thinking about food. While it's all about what there is to eat, she is still with us. She tells me she's almost done; I can come pick her up.

I wait in the parking lot of the hospital for twenty minutes. Finally, she emerges, pale and shaky, after a long, wearying day.

Back home, I watch in pleasure as she tucks into my chicken soup, the chicken curry, polony and even a slice of chocolate cake.

Eat, my mama, eat.

Each morning, I check the news for Covid updates. Flights back to Sydney are being cancelled one after the other. The problem is that there are not enough spaces in hotel quarantine. It dawns on me that I could be stuck in South Africa for six months, nine months—who knows? I feel myself being pulled by the rip of forces beyond my control, far from my little family in Sydney. Covid keeps shifting the harbour of my return.

As I lie in bed, before I am roused awake, I keep my eyes closed and imagine I am bobbing in the open water, with Coogee beach in front of me and the expanse of the ocean's reach behind me. I visualise the sensation of swell and sway underneath me, the world below the surface, alive and resplendent. My life in Sydney has taken on the quality of a dream, not quite graspable or memorable. I miss my people, Zed, Archie, my children, viscerally. And I am pining for the ocean. They are inseparable. It is a slow starvation, a leaching of my lifeforce. Swimming in the Linden public swimming pool, heated and chlorinated to the point where my skin itches, is no substitute. Memories of ordinary life, even in Sydney lockdown, make me silly with longing.

Somehow news that I am in Johannesburg gets around, and I get a call from my alma mater to ask if I will deliver the valedictory address for the matriculation class in a few weeks.

I say I'll think about it.

I don't have a single inspiring thought to share with a bunch of young people. Besides, I don't want any distractions from what is happening in front of me.

My mother asks me to get her nappies.

This must be the pivot—where the child becomes the carer, and the parent becomes the cared-for. Yet what restorative attendance there is in this reciprocating gesture, for all that our parents have given us over our lifetimes. I make my way to the chemist, glad I am here to execute these small chores for my mother, rather than being uselessly so far away, a face on an iPhone or a WhatsApp message in the night. I want things to do; I want to be deployed. My hands ache for tasks.

My father is calmer when my mother is by his side as they navigate the universe that is 60 The Braids Road, retracing the well-worn route between the loungeroom, kitchen, dining room and bedroom. Without her, he is undone.

The day after chemo, she is weak with exhaustion, but this does not deter her —she will show me how to make her ruby grapefruit jam. In the kitchen, she instructs me: how thick to cut grapefruits—skin on; not to add sugar until the pulp has boiled for an hour. She shows me the consistency of the jam by lifting a spoon, so I know when it's done. This is a rare moment; one I travelled a long way for; my mother is teaching me, and I am learning from her. It is a long day of checking on the bubbling pot every half an hour and stirring so it doesn't stick. In the end, we burn it slightly, so the jam is a little on the bitter and dark side. Dad, with his beautiful script, handwrites labels for the six bottles—we call it MoJo marmalade, for Mom and Jo. It is almost too precious to eat.

Friends offer to take me for a hike in the Magaliesberg mountains with the promise of a swim under a waterfall. It means I will be gone for the whole day. When I guiltily broach it with my mother, she says, 'Go, it will be good for you.' She probably needs a break from me, too.

It is an overcast morning as we drive out of Johannesburg, and as the city recedes, the wings of my heart unfurl. My friends have access to a private reserve, and we are the only people on the trails, ablaze with succulents, as pebbles crunch beneath our shoes, proteas rear like totem poles, and from height and distance, the world is sky and light, and we are wonderfully looking down on the shimmering marvel of everything far and blue and remote. We swim in pools of the clearest water. *Just wait till we get to the top,'* they tell me. At our destination, the waterfall in front of me is a cliché, Nature-as-you-always-wish-it-would-be. I am almost manic with desire, and strip to swim naked in the icy pool of water so sweet and pure as it pours straight from the mountain. We eat a packed picnic of hard-boiled eggs, shelled and peeled, dolloped with mayonnaise and salt and pepper.

I am rewilded, restored and returned to myself, ready to be my mother's support person as she tackles the week of chemo that lies ahead.

CHAPTER 12

Two days after the infusion, the nausea and headache kick in.

My mother writhes, moans, groans from unbearable side effects. Her eyes are wide, like a terrified bird, at the shocking intensity of it, the agony. I sit with my father beside her, as we urge her to drink, drink, drink, protect the kidneys, flush them out. These are the instructions for the days after chemo. Oh, God she is trying, trying so hard, but she cannot even keep down a sip. As the day wears on, she vomits. I look at my dad and we are both thinking the same thing: should she be on a drip? Carolyn is not here; she's in the bush without telephone reception. Who can we ask?

Watching her, watching my dad, watching my dad watching her, I am impaled at every turn. My mother tells him to stop nagging her. But he is nagging her for her life. If we can just get past these few days while the chemo wears off, she will have three weeks before the next infusion. But I cannot wrestle free of the thought—how much suffering is worth that small island of joy? There must be an equation, a moment where the balance tips one way. How can she be expected to endure this torture with each consecutive round—there are five more scheduled? We keep trying to reach Carolyn to ask her advice.

Finally, we get a frantic text from the bush—Carolyn has been wandering around desperately looking for a signal. She insists we must get Mom dripped up for the night. My mother can barely lift her head, but she makes it clear she doesn't want to go to hospital. No, we can't listen to what she wants. It's not her call, is it? What about her dignity?

Her wishes? We phone doctors and the ambulance service.

I pack her a bag with nappies, talcum powder, face cream, toothbrush, slippers and a fresh nightie. Two burly men in Hazmat suits arrive. They insist she wears a facemask—and I want to scream that it's cruel with such nausea coursing through her, but these are the Covid protocols. The men bring her down the stairs, flanking her one on each side, and help her into the ambulance. Then, she is gone.

Suddenly, it is just me and my father alone in the house. A bottle of whiskey. A conversation.

'My perfect life is gone,' he says.

He tells me again about what it was like to be an eight-year-old boy, knowing his mother was leaving him. He sits in his big armchair, and looks into a distance I cannot see into, speaking about the time he came so close to dying three years ago.

'She has looked after me so completely,' he says, 'attending to my every need…You wouldn't believe how she looks after me.'

But I would. She has done the same for me in the past. In this time, he says, he has come to love and know her as she truly is.

'What took so long?' I ask.

'It takes time to really know someone. She is such a good person.'

It's a big love story between them.

He keeps speaking, and I keep listening. He tells me how they share the same likes and dislikes and tastes in everything. He talks me through their rituals of their 5 pm dinners; how she wants to be upstairs and in bed, earlier and earlier; how much crap TV she watches while he tries to read, and how her cat Smudge must be locked in by a certain time, otherwise she gets frantic.

'I wonder if she will want to continue with this treatment. If it were me, I wouldn't.'

I nod. Who could argue with that?

As darkness falls, it is time to set the security alarm on the house, but of course, Dad has no idea how to do it. We find the remote and I press all the buttons—which promptly sets off the alarm. The phone rings, and I explain to the security company that my mother, the-one-who-knows-the-code, is not here. It is only a matter of minutes before the doorbell rings—it is a pair of armed guards from the security company, and I explain all over again, through my mask, that my mother, my sick-with-cancer-and-chemo mother, my in-hospital-nauseous-mother, the one-who-knows-the-code, is not here. A guard comes inside and shows me which buttons to press to arm the house. We thank him, he leaves, we set the alarm. It is a comedy of tragic errors. I make notes for Dad. He will not survive being this useless.

As I go through all these motions, I remember with a startle that just a week ago, I was in the Magaliesberg. I swam naked in the clearest pools. I stood under a waterfall. I saw and touched the beauty of this world, and it touched me back. This is a very different kind of Sunday. We are slowly being weaned into what missing my mother feels like, how her presence is everywhere, how big she is in all our lives. But we are also learning about how we will want to die when our dying comes. We are watching, we are wondering. We don't want her to suffer. Not for us.

Then my father says something I will come back to, over and over again, when this moment is long behind us. He speaks it out loud, like a wish or a spell. He wishes something would come and take her from left field, a heart attack, something sudden so she wouldn't have to go through the trauma of this treatment and the degeneration of the cancer taking over.

I tell him we are all facing endings. We are all approaching this grief together, from different sides.

I stay the night with my father. I sleep in Carolyn's old room, where the pictures hang skew, the windowsill is caked with dust, the bed feels itchy and scratchy, there is no bedside light, the cushions are all frilled and I am surrounded by photographs of my children as babies, Laura as a bride, Carolyn's graduation, reminders of the length and breadth of the happinesses this house has held. The old, fraying, breaking bits of things that hang—the curtains, the cloth over the bedside table, the doctor's screen. Even with the big clearing out my parents did a few years back, this place is overwhelmed with disrepair; there has been no upkeep or updating or holding together. It has all just devolved.

I think about how yesterday my mother apologised for ruining our day. She's sorry that her cancer treatment is getting in the way of our relaxing weekend.

What is it like, I wonder, to be at the centre of it all?

In the morning, we call the hospital to hear that my mother had a horrible night. Her nausea is not yet under control. I leave a message for her oncologist to ask what can be done.

'Come, Dad, let's get out of the house,' I say. We take a slow drive around Johannesburg. We pass through Yeoville—a place I lived for two years when I was in my twenties, but it is difficult to remember the Bohemian leftie-hippy vibe of those days amidst the current chaos there. My father sighs and reminisces.

Later, we are allowed to visit my mother in hospital; Covid rules, one at a time, fully masked and hand-sanitised. She is wan, exhausted to a point of lethargy. It takes so much energy to receive visitors. We don't stay long.

Back at the house, my father looks at me properly for the first time as if he's only just seen me, and asks, 'How are you?'

I break apart and can't help the tears that have been waiting to be cried. I sob and sob. I tell him that we know how hard this is for him, but, 'Dad,' I say, 'we are losing a mother.'

My father pauses at the word 'losing.'

'That's what's happening?' It is a statement dressed as a question. He knows the answer. In many ways my father knows this truth better than I do. He walked this path as a thirteen-year-old boy who'd missed the care of a mother for five years as she convalesced from one heart attack to the other, from one stint in a nursing home to the other until she died for good.

I see something in him shift as the word moves from my lips to his ears.

Here is where things change. In our language. In how we speak. In how we move from magical to realistic thinking. We stop looking at butterfly resuscitation as a 'good sign.' We try to make a home in a place where butterflies die.

'Come to terms.' 'Resign oneself.' To learn to understand and accept something.

'Dad, its stage four ovarian cancer…'

I hate the words. I detest my utterance.

I realise as I overhear myself that I am saying these words so I can hear them too.

Not hear them. Know them. *Come to terms with.*

We all just need to know where we are.

In Arabic there is a word, *Ya'aburnee.* Literally translated, it means 'you bury me.' It's used by lovers to express the hope that you will die first, and the person you love will outlive you, because without them, life would be unbearable for you. Though it's regarded as an expression of love—I begin to think that if you really, truly love someone, you hope to be the one to bury them. Loving someone means not wanting to inflict the pain of your death on them.

Upstairs, I remove the curtains from Carolyn's old room. They are in tatters and pouring down dust. I find new pure cotton sheets from the linen cupboard that mom has been saving—for what? For when? I remake the bed with them. Everything is in shreds. You touch something and it disintegrates.

My father tires me out with all the things he can't find and can't remember where he left. I worry about how bent over he is; his centre of gravity doesn't keep him stable. He's just a wobble, a stagger. But one thing I can take credit for is teaching him how to arm and disarm the house. He stresses when Smudge is not inside. When he speaks to mom on the phone, he can't lie. We tried, he tells her. But that cat does not respond to being called. I know she will be fretting all night long about it.

Dad sets off the alarm for a second time by going outside to look for Smudge again.

After three weeks, I feel nauseous with homesickness for my life back in Sydney.

From Carolyn's room I hear my father on the phone to my mother in hospital. I am standing at the foot of the bed while he's talking to her. She is confused about the time of day, about where she is. I hear her voice telling my father she is 'downstairs watching TV.'

I have that bizarre reaction when something terrifying happens. I laugh. Of course, it is the furthest thing from funny, but my nervous system responds that way. It is her becoming not-her. It is the fraying of the edges, the inching of the extinguishment. It is horrifying. The worry digs its nails into my father's face.

We make calls, we speak to the ward sister. We are told my mother must go for an MRI to rule out any concussion or other strange brain activity. Each new bit of information feels like being slammed by a wave against a rock.

Dad and I get into a fight because I call a nursing company to organise extra help for the weekends when he and mom are alone in the house. He tells me I am not to control their lives—they're fine without help. I shout at him to stop being so selfish, that my sisters and I are worried sick about them in the house.

'Mom is sick,' I howl. 'And you can't look after her by yourself.'

I leave the house in a fury to go swim in the Linden pool, pounding out those laps.

My mother has the greenest eyes. I have always been in awe of her beauty. As a child, I sometimes could not believe she belonged to me. It was partly the magnificence of the sea green eyes which she alone possessed and didn't pass down to any of her daughters. Now in hospital, with all the strict protocols and gatekeepers between us, I feel the challenge to my right of access to my own mother. I am allowed all of five minutes with her in the ward.

She's brutally bruised all over from where they've stuck needles in her for drips and other infusions, and I can barely look at these marks on her body. She seemed so well just a week ago, before the poison of this 'treatment' messed with her. I don't know that it is right to subject oneself to this torture, which, instead of extending our lives, just seems to give us more dying time.

Now I cannot help but notice that her eyes are the bluest blue.

'Can I show you how blue your eyes are?'

'My eyes have always been green,' she says.

'Mama, they've gone blue, I swear.'

She allows me to take a few photos; despite how much she hates photos of herself. I enlarge one to show her. She looks at the picture, and her response is inscrutable. I wonder what she is seeing. Something is different, beyond the change in her eye colour. There is a strange innocence to her. A childlike vulnerability, a sweetness. A softness is emerging through her brittleness. She still looks shaky. It's as if the barriers of her personality have been peeled away, and I can see her more purely.

She tells me with pride that the nurses said, 'You have three beautiful daughters.' She smiles, and I squeeze her hand.

Dad calls me late at night asking for instructions on how to operate the TV remotes. I try, but I am not trained to give tech support. It is a disaster. Oh well, he says, 'I'll just have to read.'

The next day he announces that he needs to learn how 'The Money' works. He tells me he never imagined he could do anything without my mother, but that perhaps he has reservoirs of strength he never knew about. I don't mean to undermine his good intentions, but if it was too late for my mother to engage her spiritual muscles, we are way past my father learning the difference between a bill and a tax return. We are all too old and too wise to be this naïve.

'I am looking into the abyss,' he says, and then, 'My time with your mother is precious. All I have with her is now.'

Something is loosening in him.

'Dad, it is a two-to-five-year prognosis. If all goes well, if the chemo works…' I speak these words numbly. My brain knows they are true. I am uttering them to the parts of me that have their fingers in their ears and are lah-dee-dahing, *don't-want-to-know-ing*.

I see my father absorbing this news, one small human task at a time. Arm the house. Switch on the TV. Get the cat inside. Keep the cat inside. Feed the cat. Everything she does and has always done, he will have to learn. Practicality is the stairway to deep knowing. We descend, step-by-step, holding on to each other as the world we have always known recedes and we fumble towards this new place of how-will-we-go-on?

Theo calls Dad and says mom must continue with the chemo. Without it, 'she will go quickly.' We ask him how long.

'Maybe six months.'

Six months.

'I'm not ready for that,' Dad says.

I am sitting with him in the loungeroom while he talks to her on the phone from the hospital.

'I miss you,' he says.

He tells me afterwards she said, 'I miss you too.'

She in a hospital bed, him in their bed. They are practising missing each other.

CHAPTER 13

Zed is an uncannily excellent gift buyer which, let me tell you, is a highly underrated virtue in a husband. More than generosity, of which he has oodles, it speaks of someone who knows how to listen. He is not splashy or flashy or prone to what he considers ridiculous romantic gestures that involve flora shorn from their natural habitat. He considers that a waste of money. On this, he and my mother do not see eye-to-eye. Nothing pleases her more than a vase of roses or tulips, or small offerings of geraniums from her garden.

When I started ocean swimming, Zed bought me a Garmin watch, called a Fenix, with a white strap and a circle of red gold around the face. Its most fabulous feature is that it is waterproof. It measures my distance when I swim. It also has other surveillance capacities, like tracking my daily steps, calories burned and my sleep. Every morning, it offers me a sleep report. Not only the hours, but a commentary: Poor, Fair, Good or Excellent. It tells me if my sleep was well-balanced, interrupted, disturbed, if I had enough REM, if I have recovered sufficiently.

If it tells me I've had poor sleep, I am giddy all day. If it announces I've had good sleep, I feel I can tackle anything that comes my way.

I do not need my Garmin to tell me that since I arrived in South Africa, my sleep has been 'poor.' Sleep feels almost illicit, unattainable, something I once slid into with ease. Now, when it catches me, it is by surprise, it drags me under, like an anaesthetic for a few numbing hours, and when I awake, I feel disoriented, confused, *where was I?...oh... right...* and the thump of reality punches me again.

In these crammed sleep snatches, I dream wildly.

'How's your appetite? Can I bring you anything to eat?' I text my mother.

'Better thanks, fancy an omelette,' she replies.

'With cheese and onion?'

'Just cheese.'

And then, 'Two pieces of toast with butter.'

A pause. 'Chips as well.'

'What flavour?'

'Salt and vinegar.'

I make an omelette and wrap it in tinfoil, and I pack the toaster in a bag and take bread and butter with me to the hospital. I plug in the toaster and make fresh toast in her room and watch her tuck in. She complains it's too salty. This has to be a first. It's odd, completely out of character. My mother has always sprinkled salt like confetti over food.

Everything I know about her is shifting. Panic pecks at me.

When she comes home from hospital, I volunteer to sleep in the house and be 'the nurse on duty' for a night while we organise a trained carer from a nursing organisation who can start the following day. Is it forgivable to admit that even as I do, I am deeply resistant? I know I will not sleep, but I need to be there. Part of me wants to, but I also wish I didn't have to. I feel this rent in me, to be the good daughter, to stay and take care of my mother, even as I long to run away.

To see this flaw is not flattering. It is a source of hot shame. I am not Etty Hillesum, who wrote, 'Where you happen to find yourself, be there with your whole heart. If your heart is elsewhere, you won't give enough to the community in which you happen to be, and the community will be the poorer for it.' No, I am not even close.

The Tibetan monk Thich Nhat Hahn once said, 'When you love someone, the best thing you can offer is your presence. How can you love if you are not there?' In my wrung-out state, I am trying, but I am not all gathered here. I am scattered. Half in this moment, and half-way escaped, longing for things to be different. So much for all my spiritual practice over the decades. I am failing horribly. There is no comfort in seeing myself so clearly.

I lie in the uncomfortable bed in Carolyn's room, between the new sheets. I have a restless, resentful night, my ears attuned for any sounds that might mean my mother needs me. I dream I am having chemo. I have breast cancer in my left breast and am being hooked up to a machine while the treatment is being administered by a young woman. I realise that 'cancer treatment' is 'in' and everyone's having it, like Botox, and I wonder if I really need it and whether I should be putting myself through it.

Then I dream I live in a mansion, a huge castle, that has a gate like a fort, and the gate is struggling to close because a branch of a tree is caught in it. I wonder why I have chosen to live in such an enormous home, when I love my little flat by the sea so much.

A young nurse from a nursing agency arrives to help over the weekend. I pack my belongings into my mother's car and move to my friend

Tanya's home, a six-minute drive from my parents'. I need to step away and have some time to myself. Carolyn sees how tearful and ragged I am. She warns me that I have given too much all at once and that I need to pace myself.

In Tanya's home, I have the best sleep since I arrived in South Africa. Nine hours and forty-five minutes of Good, Deep, Refreshing Sleep, my Garmin tells me. Being in a space that is energetically unconnected to what is happening in my family gives me a chance to replenish myself and recharge. I take Carolyn's cautionary words to heart and try to mete out my giving to my parents in small, manageable doses.

In between, I take myself off for breakfast at a café and do an online Pilates class around Tanya's plunge pool. I scribble a few notes for the valedictory address I have agreed to do, before I drive over to my parents, filled up, resourced. I arrive strong and with a smile. But my mother and father look bleak in their unmoving positions on their respective chairs in the loungeroom.

On this morning, my mother asks, 'Can I have my credit card back?'

I am bewildered. I've been holding onto it so I can do all the grocery and pharmaceutical shopping. She cannot decide whether to surrender complete control over the shopping or not. Perhaps it's too much of an admission that she is losing reign over such things as the eggs and milk in the fridge. I hand back the credit card, unsure how I will do the shopping now.

'I had a bad night,' she says when I ask her how she is. 'I started thinking about whether I'll be able to carry on with the chemo, and that I 'won't make old bones.' Everything feels bleak.'

My father can barely speak while she admits these fears. She'd tossed and turned through the night, not wanting to wake my dad.

'I wish you had,' he mumbles.

'Mom, you can always call me in the middle of the night,' I say. 'I can talk about these things.'

'I don't like to talk about them,' she says.

Tanya's house is serene in the way minimal spaces are. I am reminded of how much I fail at living this way. Here, with all the free surfaces, white walls and open space, I start to feel. The lack of clutter opens me to myself. In this gap, the ache of missing my children burns. Without any distractions or mess, my longing for them chokes me. It's not just the distance. It's the separation piggybacking on the backlog of months of lockdown which forced us apart. I know only this: a mother should not be kept from her children. The ache turns to anger. Then tears.

As I lie in the large comfy bed in Tanya's house, I think about the carer we have employed who is spending her weekend at 60 The Braids Road who probably has a family she is shorn from, to be on call if my mother needs her. She likely has children who miss her.

I turn onto my side, sobbing, I don't know who for.

CHAPTER 14

My computer is propped on my parents' bed as they watch Jess on the screen. I am seated at my mother's dressing table, and I watch them, watching her. A strangled feeling rises in my throat. Over Zoom, Jess is singing five of my mother's favourite songs.

Seeing my mother and daughter reunited, even like this, is almost too much to bear. For the first eighteen months of her life, Jess spent every afternoon singing nursery rhymes, running around the garden and watching *Telytubbies* with her Nana. I have never seen my mother happier than those eighteen months when we lived just around the corner. All the unmet longings and absences of my childhood were healed when I watched her as a first-time grandmother. It was as if she'd finally shaken the despairs of motherhood and could give herself completely to the task of being present for a grandchild. Witnessing it was a kind of beautiful repair.

When she was thirteen, Jess had asked me, 'Why did you take us out of South Africa? Why did you take me away from my grandparents and my aunts and cousins?'

Distance from.

Can't get to.

Out of reach.

When a child asks, you have a choice: shield them by telling them a falsehood or a half-truth or offer the truth. We assume our children don't 'know' the secrets we imagine we are so adept at keeping from them. But somewhere in their mitochondria, they know it all. Every brutality, tragedy and sorrow felt in the ancestral line sings into our children's blood, through their dreams, desires, beliefs and hopes and hatches into strange and exotic anxieties, addictions or phobias.

There it was—my chance to tell her why Zed and I reluctantly, agonisingly, decided to leave South Africa, the land where she and her brother were born, took their first steps, were first-loved and familied.

I explained. At least, I tried. The violence. My anxiety. That her godmother had been gang raped. How my father had said to me, 'Get your children out of here.' How we'd left everything behind—our home in Cape Town, my work as an expert in domestic violence, their grandparents on both sides, four aunts, six cousins, friends, life-as-we-knew-it. We'd hoped we were giving her and her brother a safer life.

She listened quietly to every word. And then she said, 'Mum, there's violence everywhere.'

'That's true, my love.' I wiped my eyes. 'We thought we'd done the right thing. But maybe we were wrong. I'm so sorry.'

We can never anticipate the negative, unintended consequences of our most carefully intended actions.

Notwithstanding Zed's observation about her sad eyes, my mother often expressed that Australia was a heaven, a place far away from all the tension of the poverty, violence and stresses of South Africa. On the few occasions when she came to visit us on her own and stayed in one of the kids' rooms, I saw her truly relax. When Zed got home from work, she'd pour us all a glass of wine (the cheap Jacob's Creek was her favourite) and lay out olives, chips and dips on the loungeroom table. She'd laugh at all his jokes, encouraging his silliness. She'd say, 'Let me get that for you,' if I so much as admired a sweater, shoes or earrings. She'd splurge on new wine glasses, a light for the loungeroom, and whatever the kids needed or expressed a passing desire for, spoiling each of us. She went crazy for the seafood, sushi and doner kebabs. We ate oysters and prawns from the local fishmongers. She loved Kmart, Big W, Peters of Kensington, the Fish Market, and even Eastgardens shopping centre. She was always keen for the walk from Coogee to Clovelly and the loop around Centennial Park before we'd pick up the kids from school. She was undemanding, content to just hang around with us when I apologised that it couldn't be much fun for her. She'd cook curries for us, her special bolognaise sauce and watch whatever TV the kids enjoyed in the afternoons. She bought slabs of beer and the best whiskey for Zed and filled my grocery cupboard with olive oils and marinated vegetables.

She worried about leaving my dad on his own. 'He's a bit useless,' she'd say good-naturedly, and she'd call him every day to find out if he'd taken his medication, how the animals were doing and if he'd paid the gardener with the money she'd left in a clearly marked envelope on the dresser in the entrance hall.

When she laughed, it always stopped me. I wanted to hold onto it. In those moments, a sense of her being someone else, besides how we knew her, bubbled out. It was strange and magic, a precious enigma, as if a flap of inner life had peeled away, revealing someone she might have been; or maybe in essence was, but so seldom got the chance to be.

On this bleak day, with my mother back from hospital, her granddaughter Jess across unnavigable oceans, sings five songs, including my mother's two requests, 'Hallelujah' and 'Imagine'.

Jess cries at the end. But her singing cheers my mother and father up. My ribcage cradles a jungle of hurts.

Zed texts me to let me know that in Australia, they are trialling home quarantine for returning overseas travellers for the next few weeks. It means I may not have to be holed up in a hotel room for two weeks when I get back. I can be in my own apartment, with my own things, with Zed and Archie. I crumble with relief, as an invisible yoke falls away. The many thousands of dollars I save, I can put towards a ticket to return next year.

I check my calendar—I have been in South Africa a month. Two more to go.

I open Jess's third letter, *Late September*, in which she writes she hopes by the time I'm reading this, Sydney is out of lockdown (it isn't) and that I've been able to bring some light into my family.

All I've brought is her singing to them, and a garden full of succulents.

'What if I teach you and mom how to use the computer to order food online?' I suggest to Dad.

I have only been part of this tag team of sisters for a few weeks, but I've noticed how much pressure my sisters face daily. My dad is adamant that it's not a big deal to impose these tasks on us. 'We're old, and it's your job as our kids. Who else can we turn to?' he demands.

I argue, and he gets angry at me. We shout at each other, and I leave in a huff, almost as if I'm infuriated that my mother is so unwell that she cannot learn something new.

When we are alone, Carolyn says, 'Sometimes you just have to leave them to deal with their own emotions.'

Alone at Tanya's house, I pull the net off her pool and immerse myself in the water. I close my eyes and imagine I am out beyond the Coogee Surf Life Saving Club, bobbing in the water, far from shore. I sink into the quiet and try to roll towards this inevitable circumstance: *my mother will leave us*. It is an impossible thought. She is leaving us with every hour that passes. I cannot stop it or pause it or ask for a moment to catch my breath. It will do what it's doing, ready-or-not-here-it-comes. But every day I try to befriend it a little more. It's a haunting refrain under each moment, being with what is leaving us.

I wish, wish, wish for her—and also for us—that she had worked towards some kind of spiritual understanding of this subsiding; that death was not such a horror to her. I only see her swaying with distraction, medicating against emotion. And with every numbing, she pushes us further away. There is nowhere to congregate in this anaesthetising jungle of *God-help-me-not-to-feel*.

I hope I have been offering olive branches, reaching out to be someone she can confide in if she needs to. I must believe she will find a way to surrender, to be light with it, to soften into what is happening. I want her to break away soft and free on the wings of a thousand blessings.

Only now, when time is so slender, and the hours so precious, do I catch myself, after all these weeks of trying too hard.

These are all *my* needs, what *I* want; they are not what she wants.

I must prepare myself for her to turn her head away from it, till the end.

Who am I to judge?

She is teaching me. It's just not the lesson I imagined—that this is not how I would choose to die.

The next morning, with a shopping list in hand, I take myself off to the African market at Rosebank to look for an outfit for the valedictory event. I wander through the shops and market, trying on clothes before I attend to the list of things my mother has asked me to get.

Back at the house, she complains that the cheese I bought isn't the right one. I had spent fifteen minutes looking through all the cheeses before picking the one I thought must surely be it.

I suddenly feel exhausted from her complaining, even though I know it's her outlet. Even when I arrive at the house with samosas, rotis and sushi, all her favourite foods, she barely says thanks anymore. Carolyn brings her a brownie and trout. We all try to appease her with food, to tempt her back into life.

The horror is dawning that the old ways are not working anymore.

CHAPTER 15

Carolyn and I lie side by side on her bed, head-to-head, not head to toe like we used to when we were little and played Tickle-Toe. I am spending the night with her while her husband is away for a few nights. We scratch her cats, Dusty and Miro, who lie between us, their softness a cushion against the gunmetal truths hard up against our backs.

The results of mom's new blood tests are back. The cancer markers have doubled since her last round of chemo. Under my one hand, Dusty's purr throbs. Carolyn holds my other hand as I try to absorb the information. I see in my sister's face the gravity of this result.

I swallow a tranquilliser and close my eyes, waiting for it to work. It does nothing. My thoughts are a-scramble. Next to Carolyn, I lie awake as the hours of the night tick over. At 2 am, I go to the loungeroom and call my family. Zed and Aidan pick up, but talking to them just makes me feel lonelier. I have caught them in the middle of their day, and it is impossible to impart the darkness of this hour. I also don't want to seem too pathetic, though I really am. I wander through the house looking for Dusty and find him asleep in the spare room. I cuddle him to me, letting his purrs reverberate through me, this oblivious, dreaming ball of fluff, and then I cry. I cry and cry. This ending is coming sooner than I thought.

Back in bed, I take another tranquilliser wanting to be anaesthetised against all feeling. I wake to dawn's first light, feeling drunk, with not nearly enough sleep in me.

Carolyn and I walk to a local café, solemn and quiet on this beautiful spring morning. We drink enormous coffees, and despite our poor appetites, we share a smoked salmon sandwich, which is like sawdust in our mouths. We discuss how to break the news to mom. We agree it is not right for it to fall on Carolyn. She is, despite her medical training, a daughter first, not mom's doctor. She doesn't know what the blood results mean in terms of treatment options. She needs to speak to the oncologist. Maybe there is a different intravenous chemo, even the deadly one that affects the heart.

My cat Tanaka had kidney disease for many years, which the vet told me would finally claim her. I knew for a long time that her time was running out, and I stayed as close to the leaving as I could. Every purr, every pat, every night she slept at my feet, was ablaze with preciousness. Before we put her down, I held her wrapped in a blanket through the night, watching her sleep, telling her how much I loved her and would miss her. She died in my arms. She let me be with her through the leaving.

I am angry with myself. I have been blisteringly, blindly naïve. Toxically positive. I had faith my mother would fight this longer, she'd respond better to the treatment, we'd have more time. And what about those bloody Turkey Tail mushroom tablets?

All I know is that I must stay here, by her side, until we have to say goodbye.

Carolyn texts Theo to tell him the news and ask if he will relay it to mom—not as a friend, but as one of her doctors. This wonderful, kind and compassionate man says he will. Carolyn is tearful with relief.

Later, I am in the loungeroom with my folks when he calls. I watch and overhear her side of the conversation.

'I see,' I hear her say. 'Okay... mmm...'

She seems stunned.

When she puts the phone down, she doesn't say anything. But I know what she's been told. She gets up to go to the bathroom. My father looks after her, at the closed door, fear etched on his face.

First, there's the telling: the cancer markers have doubled.

And there's what that means.

I don't know how the one plus ones work here. I need someone to spell it out for me. This is not a language I know or understand.

I surreptitiously text Theo. I ask him to be frank with me. I need to know what time is left so I can decide whether to go back to Sydney in eight weeks or stay here. If there are only months left, there is no point in my going back all that way only to have to come back when this cancer has colonised her entirely.

Theo explains, the cancer is 'out of control.' He spells it out: the chemo is not working. The 'prognosis is very guarded,' he texts.

I ask, 'Please explain.'

'Frankly, prognosis is not great.'

'Six months?' I ask.

'Impossible to say, sorry,' he replies.

He also writes as an afterthought, 'HOWEVER (in caps) there always remains hope, no matter how dark things appear.'

Is this what doctors do?

What force is hope against this mutating disease, advancing like an unstoppable military power? I have no space in me for false hope. I'm not a child.

The realisation that we are literally counting down months, weeks, days, hours, enters me like an anaesthetic. I feel weak in my elbows, my knees, as I've been kicked in all my folding places.

Mamelah, my little mama.

Every day, I do all my crying before I pull up in front of 60 The Braids Road. I check my eyes for tell-tale mascara streaks in the rearview mirror before I slap my cheeks and hoist my mouth into a smile so I can walk through the front door that is never locked, with a 'Hi Mom and Dad,' and a lilt in my voice. That is my job.

I write letters to my mother, making notes of each moment dragging us like a rip toward our imminent loss. I cry and do Pilates and count the days down on my calendar.

When I was in Australia, all I wanted was to be here. Now that I'm here, I just want to go back. I don't know how to gather myself, to tether my resistance, recall my need to flee and be gone. Right now, I am doing exactly what my mother is—I am dancing like crazy to avoid being present to what is unfolding.

Our family crowds around the one end of the dining room table with my laptop in the centre. Laura joins the meeting from her home. Our parents' financial advisor pops up on the screen. My mother is feeling shaky again today. Anxiety, maybe low sodium, or a cocktail of both. Each day her colours fade into that terrible non-colour as terminal illness takes hold.

The discussion is about numbers: how much my parents have in their estate, how much they need to live on, and how the money will be managed 'if one spouse dies.' My mother's face is stony throughout.

It is a tough conversation, couched in subtext: who will control the finances and pay the bills when she is no longer here to take care of all that. Handing it over to my father is like giving a five-year-old a credit card and wishing him luck.

My mother doesn't say much. But I sense how emotional she is beneath her controlled veneer. I do most of the talking. The financial advisor gently says, in a tone he has perfected, that he needs all kinds of documents—the title deeds for 60 The Braids Road, originals of one thing and another. She nods. Only she knows where everything is filed.

The pain everyone is feeling is subsumed into the tasks. I know there is agony here, and that later, I will feel it. For now, we are all anaesthetised, drunk on despair. Even so, I sort of marvel that, as a family, I think we are doing okay. I cannot imagine how impossible a conversation this would be for some families; it would bring up so many tricky dynamics and tensions.

With the calamity of loss bearing down from all sides, it feels wrong to be speaking about money now. Yet we discuss what percentage the executor will take. I have no clue what 'a reasonable percentage' is—I just agree with whatever my parents want. I cannot find a shred of energy to exert around money.

Laura says no matter what, we three sisters mustn't fight, and she is right.

After our meeting ends, my mother turns to me and says, 'When I saw Laura on the screen, I realised how close the two of us have become over the past few years and how much I love her.'

Here it is—a luminous moment. Something real and true.

'Tell her that, mom,' I encourage. 'She needs to hear that from you. Do it. Do it now.'

From the corner of my eye, I see her on her phone sending a text to Laura. This, I remind myself, is why I came.

In Tanya's home, I try to be an unobtrusive guest; fit neatly into her world, not to make too much noise, disrupt her fridge or leave a trace of myself. It exhausts me. It is easy to overstay our welcome anywhere, no matter how hospitable the host. At times, I feel petulant, bratty with need as I attend to everyone else's. My sisters have the comfort and refuge of their homes, lives, work, families and routines around which this grief is seeping like water around rocks. I am alone, like a polar bear floating on a piece of ice out into the middle of nowhere as the icebergs of my world melt.

It is hard not to feel lost or orphaned even before my mother has gone.

A week after Theo's phone call, my mother announces that she wants 'Indian for lunch.' Curry—it's not for the feeble or ailing. It demands a robust appetite, with its rich flavours and deeply spiced sauces. But we jump to her every wish and whim and order takeaways from an Indian restaurant around the corner. We are frantically convening, making a ceremony of The Takeaway, indulging all her wants and tastes. Carolyn sets up the table outside with the chair covers and winds out the awning to tempt my mother to come outside and sit in the sun. My mother tries to make a show of enjoying herself and manages, but only for a few minutes, before she says it's too hot. She just wants to sit on her round, squishy bagel pillow on the couch in front of the television. But if that's where she's happy, I must let it be. Later, I find her and Dad watching *Squid Game*—a horrific, bloodthirsty TV series. With time running out, this is what she wants to fill her mind with. Again, I grab myself. I must stop judging her.

And I sit down on the couch, and I watch this ghastliness with them.

CHAPTER 16

I take the morning off to drive to Muldersdrift so I can swim in a dam. I need to move my limbs and be held by a wild body of water. It is not the ocean; I cannot see the bottom, the water is brackish, full of weeds, but it is alive, and it does the job, even though it seems wrong, sinful to spend even a moment away from my mother.

When I return from my swim, revived, I sit in the loungeroom and watch the Dolly Parton documentary with my folks. We all end up in quiet tears as she sings, 'I will always love you.' Dad constantly strokes mom's hand, and eventually she asks him to please stop, it's annoying her. Watching the two of them, I am stung as those words settle into me. *Please stop.*

In the car, we speak about what she's watching on TV, a new movie with Melissa McCarthy called *The Starling*. It is early morning, and I am driving my mother to the hospital for another round of blood tests. When the results come through, she will see her oncologist and we'll find out if there are any other treatment options. She is trying so hard to be brave—chatting about inanities when there is so much on her mind she won't share or speak of. But she reeks of fear.

I return to the house to spend the morning with my father.

'When your mother dies,' he says, 'I'm not moving from this house.'

Now he speaks of *when* not *if.* This is a tilt; he has processed what is happening. I can barely breathe from the sadness.

Later, my mother sends a text to say she is going to have another chemo treatment. It means her blood tests must have shown she is well enough. This is good news, isn't it? An hour later, she is done and asks me to pick her up. On the way home, she says she feels like a toasted cheese and tomato sandwich from one of her favourite cafes, and of course, anything, anything, anything she wants… I drop her back at 60 The Braids and head off with my toasted sandwich assignment.

Later, I help my mother sort out the documents the executor needs. We make little piles on the dining room table, weighted down with candles.

Carolyn lets us know that the cancer markers have come down from 1182 to 826. They've come down… come down… everyone is buoyed by this news. Encouraged by my daily swims, Dad gets in the pool and emerges, shivering. But the cold water invigorates him. He is rallying in some strange way.

So, our little family continues to lurch from blood test to blood test, praying, hoping, willing those numbers to come down, stay the same, do anything but go up, so we have a little more time.

Just when I was sliding into despair, hope creeps back in.

The executor says thanks, he'll have a coffee with two sugars.

We are sitting around the dining room table having a family meeting, asking him questions about my mother's will, what to do with the house and what will happen when she is no longer here. He gives us a list of documents we must find to put in a file so that everything is in one place.

He suggests we should let her know what we each want from the house. It feels covetous and premature to be laying claim to her things—her furniture, fridge, vases, mirrors, lamps, statues. I'm glad I live so far away. I can't shlep things across the ocean. I have her recipes. I will take a jar of MoJo marmalade back home. I don't want or need anything else.

The next day I wake up with a headache and a sniffle.

Never in the history of a headache and a sniffle has there been such panic. What if it's Covid?

Carolyn picks me up and drives me to her lab. She marches me straight through reception with her doctor's lanyard, instructs one of the lab technicians to take a swab and personally delivers the swab to her lab at the hospital. The result comes back within two hours. Negative. A blessed reprieve.

I spend the day resting in Tanya's guest bedroom, not wanting to bring even a minor sniffle near my mother's collapsing immune system. As I lie in bed unable to visit my mother, I realise how drained I am from the past weeks. It takes an energy I no longer have to be in other people's spaces.

I talk this through with Zed, and with his encouragement, I book an Airbnb for six nights, just so I can be alone.

The news from the Braids Road is bleak as the nausea from the chemo kicks in.

I call Dad on WhatsApp. He points the phone in my mother's direction, and I see her, a crumpled figure in the bed, a glass of Coke undrunk on her bedside table.

He has been sitting vigil by her side, reading *The Man Who Mistook His Wife for A Hat*. He tells me he's given up on *Ulysses*, because 'life is too short.'

As my eyes take in this sorrowful scene, I wonder if she is nudging nearer the time when she will look at all of us and say, 'I am done with this'? How much more of this can she put herself through, and for what? For more Netflix? For Dad?

'I just wish your mother would drink something,' my father sighs.

I pull up in the driveway of 60 The Braids Road early the next morning. I let myself in and climb the stairs.

My mother is sitting on the edge of Dad's bed.

She is as frail as a broken bird. Whatever has been done to her has claimed her already. I gently help her take off her nightie and put on her socks. She is beyond bending or attending to these tasks. I touch her sagging, tired body. I stroke her pale face. I feel the clamminess of her yellowed skin. She insists on coming downstairs after spending the last two days in bed.

'I must come down, otherwise I'll just get weaker.'

Downstairs is where living happens—the cooking, eating, laughing, lounging, coming and going. Upstairs is where people lie sick in bed.

I don't think it's a good idea, but I help her down the stairwell, one stair at a time. In the loungeroom, I massage her neck, which is in spasm. I make her a hot water bottle and rest it on her shoulders to relieve some of the pain. She can barely talk; she is not even in the mood to watch television. I make her comfortable on the couch.

My father has an appointment at the hospital to see his urologist, so I drive him. In the car, he says, 'How long can she go on like this? At what point is her quality of life not worth this?'

Suddenly, what each of us wants ceases to matter. Here it is—my father's acceptance—and it heralds a new way of loving someone in which you love them enough to let them go, because their pain is not part of the deal. I see now how you can change what you hope for, how you renegotiate what you're asking of God in your prayers, how you can stifle your own needs and bow to the inevitable loss.

I won't say this out loud to her, but I feel it with every part of me: I don't want to see her suffer any more. I don't need her to put herself through this much longer for my sake.

When Emma was rushed to hospital, with a massive blood clot that ran from her thigh to her lung, as a nurse, she must have understood the peril of her condition. Just before she died, she turned to her husband and asked, 'Do you think that when we die, God comes down and takes our hand?'

And bless him, he replied, 'He does.'

If you visit the Royal North Shore Hospital in Sydney, you will find a hand-carved bench in the shape of a hand dedicated to her. It is called 'He does.'

I wonder whether God will come down and take my mother's hand.

Even if she doesn't believe in 'all that stuff.'

Carolyn and I spend a few hours in a shopping mall on a mission to find a small 2022 diary to fit in her bag, as my mother requested. A year of blank pages for her to fill.

We return to the house in the late afternoon where we find her lying on the couch where the light streams in on sunny days, with Smudge snuggled into the crook of her arm. I hand her the diary, 'We found just what you wanted, mom.'

She nods, in her exhausted state, reaches for her handbag, and I watch as she slips it into the side pocket. We hover; does she want or need anything? She shakes her head, eyes closed.

Only later will I reopen the door of this moment to see what was really before me. At the time, it was like this: I gaze at my poor mother and think, 'She looks deathly ill. We should leave her to rest.' The clue is right there, lulling in that observation, and the part of me that is a writer registers that were I ever to describe someone on their deathbed, this is the moment I'd conjure: withered, skin ashen, face pale, sallow, verging on something not quite here, tenuously alive. Not a shred of solace for the eye to rest upon.

Then I think, get a grip on yourself. She's just recovering from the chemo.

I kiss her on the forehead and whisper, 'See you tomorrow, mama.'

PART 3
GONE

CHAPTER 17

It's 2.07 am, according to my Garmin. I stare wide-eyed into the darkness, but sleep has escaped like a wild winged thing into the night, so I reach for my iPad. I've been watching *Jane the Virgin*, the series my mother has not stopped talking about. I do not see it coming—a failure on my part as a storyteller—but in this episode, one of the most beloved characters dies. I am furious, heartbroken. Why? No! Not him! Why him?

I sob and sob because, poor, poor Jane.

Spent, I fall asleep sometime after 4.30am.

My iPhone rings, ripping me from complicated dreams. I pick it up in a daze. I don't recognise the name. Bridget? Who is Bridget? Oh, it's the carer. It's not even 7 am.

'Hello Bridget?' my voice is croaky with no sleep.

'Jo, come quickly,' she says.

'Why, what's happened?' Panic flares in me, a scribble of dark emotion.

'Just come quick. Madam is not waking up.'

'No, no, no…'

Tanya rushes into the room in her gown, woken by my cries.

The mind becomes empty space. There are things the body does, like get dressed, pulling on the first dress the hand reaches for in the closet, time rushes like a torrent, and everything is in slow motion all at once. The teeth are brushed.

'Laura, Mom isn't waking up. I'm going to the house.' The speech from my mouth says into the phone.

Fingers fumble as they try to call Carolyn's husband. But his phone is on silent. Another fumbling to call his daughter who is staying with them. She answers, slurry with sleep.

'Sorry to call so early, it's urgent. Please wake Carolyn.'

Tanya says, 'Let me drive you, I don't want you behind a wheel in your state.'

'I'm okay.'

Somehow, the car is driven, the roads pass under the tyres, the driveway to 60 The Braids Road suddenly appears and there is the front door, a bungling for the front door key, in it goes, but no, the door is bolted from the inside. Bridget opens it, setting off the house alarm. Within seconds the phone is ringing—it's the security company to find out if there's a home invasion, and in all this, there is a mother upstairs, not waking up.

'It's okay, there's no break-in,' my voice shouts into the phone.

Then, two, three stairs at a time, legs carry me up the stairs, and there she lies, still, even paler than she was yesterday, and with Bridget now doing chest compressions, I bend down and begin mouth-to-mouth resuscitation—or some version of it—but her jaw is rigid. I force her mouth open, and try to breathe the breath inside me, into her mouth. Bridget continues pumping her chest, this slight woman, industrious, unwavering, as I try to give air to this person who is not breathing and is my mother. Sighing, groaning sounds emerge from her mouth. Oh my god, she is reviving...

Bridget says, 'Yes, yes, she is waking up.'

But no, she is so cold, stone cold.

My sisters and Jenna arrive. We gather around, hugging, sobbing.

Two men in an ambulance arrive. They ask us to leave the room, while they lay our mother on the floor and put paddles on her chest. They shock her a few times.

But she is gone. She has been for hours.

I ask them to put her back on the bed.

'It's better if she stays on the floor,' they say, but I don't care what they think is better. My mother is not lying on the floor. I insist they lift her back into her bed. Then they cover her face with a blue sheet. I pull it down to show her face, so it looks as if she is just tucked up in bed.

We sit around her. We all take turns holding her hand, kissing her and telling her we love her. When the men from the Jewish burial society come, they will whisk her away, and we will never get her back.

During this precious gap, I call Zed and the kids. I turn the camera around so they can see my mother's frozen face. They speak their tearful goodbyes.

Dad, who is sitting quietly in the chair at her dressing table, gets up and comes to stand over her. He leans down to look at her face as if he is seeing it for the first time, looking so deep and so long, we all sit there and turn away, unable to witness this moment without breaking.

Two men from the Jewish burial society arrive. They are sorry for our loss. They know what to do with a dead body. There is a protocol for this unthinkable scenario, a world about which I know nothing.

There is paperwork, which Laura offers to fill in. I am in awe of her composure. They ask us not to look as they lift her body and bring her down the stairs in a black bag. Whose idea was it to put our most precious beloved in an oversized garbage bag? Why not a handwoven shawl? A sheet? Something that involves comfort, warmth, swaddling, rather than intimating trash. My rage is a stupidity; of course plastic is necessary to avoid leakage of bodily fluids, but I recoil from this inadvertent dehumanising functionality and efficiency. They lift her onto a gurney to wheel her to the van.

At the front door, the one through which my mother walked some fifty-four years earlier before whispering, 'I love it,' Dad asks to see her again. The men unzip the bag, and he looks at her face with such tenderness I don't know that I can bear it. They ask us to walk behind as they wheel her to their van, and they slide her inside. We thank them for their godly work. Then they drive away.

We turn and go back inside.

Laura makes calls to book a gravesite, a rabbi, a time for the funeral. I could not do what she is doing. Not now. Suddenly, the burial is locked in for tomorrow at eleven. She reserves a plot next to mom's for Dad, for 'when he goes.' This cool-headedness, rationality and practicality in the middle of crisis is a competence I don't possess. She is so like our mother.

Within the hour, cousins arrive, bearing bagels and hard-boiled eggs, and the day becomes a blur. Laura and I find pillowcases in the linen cupboard, and as is the Jewish tradition during the seven days of sitting *Shiva*, which has now sprung upon us, we move through the rooms, covering all the mirrors.

Carolyn says we cannot leave Dad alone tonight. We must stay with him.

I am a fumbling mess, but suddenly I remember that I booked an Airbnb for tonight. I send a message to explain that my mother has just died, and my plans have changed. I request a cancellation and refund under these unusual circumstances.

I am utterly dumbfounded, accosted, when the owner refuses, though she's 'sorry for my loss.' Rules are rules.

I tell Carolyn that I won't be able to sleep if I stay in the house.

'No-one will have a good night's sleep tonight because our mother has just died.' She tells me I'm running away, and of course, she's right.

I am the 'visitor,' I am expected to be itinerant. I cannot claim 'home' or being needed elsewhere. I relent for this night. I will stay with Carolyn and my dad.

My father calls everyone he knows and has ever known to tell them the news.

I begin to tidy up. I collect the dozens of bottles of water dotted around the house and empty them into the garden; I throw away old jars on the kitchen counter I have been wanting to clear out for years, jars that my mother never wanted to part with. I start cleaning up like a deranged person. I cannot sit still. It is a giddy, reckless freedom, almost as if I am testing whether I will be stopped, that someone will say, 'No, you can't, put that back.'

In the kitchen, we make tea, and Bridget tells us how, at around 2 am, mom called for her, needing help to go to the toilet. She was shaky and weak, and Bridget told her she would bring her yoghurt in the morning to help her build up her strength. Then she put mom back into bed.

She must have slipped away soon after that tender encounter. While I was watching *Jane the Virgin*.

Carolyn's medical explanation is that the chemo was too much, and either her heart gave in, or she had a pulmonary embolism.

We will never know.

Upstairs in her bedroom, I find the vest my mother was wearing when she died. It smells of her, and I stuff it into my handbag. I take her nail scissors from her bedside table and a face cream from her dressing table. I stare at her side of the bed, which Bridget has neatly made and am assailed by a memory from childhood.

I was waiting on the bench for my school bus to pick me up when a large black Doberman ran into the road. It belonged to one of our classmates who lived close to the school and often roamed the school hallways, sometimes sneaking in and out of the classrooms. It bounded out into the path of a bus that had just taken off. I felt the surge of a terrible premonition. This is what happened: the front wheels of the bus smashed the dog's back legs. It tried to stand by lifting its head and front legs, just as the back wheels of the bus crushed the life out of it. It was no more than a few seconds between a living, breathing, barking creature and a bloodied mess of fur, flesh and bones.

When I was nineteen, I was on holiday in Swaziland with a girlfriend. We were staying in a hotel high up in the mountains, the only guests apart from one other family. On the first night, we were tucking into our soup and bread when, at a table across the dining hall, the grandmother began to choke. We watched as the father attempted the Heimlich manoeuvre. But within seconds, the old woman slumped and fell to the floor. As we were ushered out of the dining room by hotel staff; we saw them covering her with a tablecloth. Back in our room, we wondered what had just happened? One minute, a person was enjoying the cream of mushroom soup and a buttered dinner roll. The next, they were a corpse.

When I was once having treatment for my back with a body therapist, she told me she'd lost a child. He'd drowned, she'd said, in their swimming pool.

He'd been playing on a swing in their backyard and had somehow gotten through the locked security gate around the pool.

What she said next has never left me.

'By the time he was pronounced dead, the swing he'd been playing on was still in motion.'

Now I remember that on an overcast morning during lockdown in Coogee, I was swimming backstroke in the bay, as I sometimes did, when something smacked into me. 'Sorry,' I called out, thinking it was another swimmer—it's surprising how often you bump into others in the open water. But when I turned, I discovered it was a creature, an exquisite thing with a little mast sticking out of the water, tentacled like an octopus. I realised, Oh my god, *it's a cuttlefish*. It bobbed around me as I examined it, enchanted.

Only later did it dawn on me that a live cuttlefish doesn't behave that way. It must have been dying or even dead to bump into me the way it did.

Even when we think we know how close death hovers, the moment it comes, we realise we did not know.

CHAPTER 18

On the day of my mother's funeral, the rabbi's beard is bothering me.

We'd requested that he wear a see-through visor instead of a mask so that Carolyn can lipread and follow the proceedings. Even so, his beard is so unruly, it hides his mouth. It becomes the focus of my rage.

Earlier, we'd met as a family in the office of the Jewish Burial Society, where a man explained the proceedings that were about to unfold: we would have our shirts cut to symbolise the tearing of our souls. My dad would recite the mourner's prayer when the coffin came out.

'I also want to say the prayer for my mother,' I'd insisted.

'It's not allowed by traditional Jewish law,' Laura said.

'I don't care.' My blood thundered in my chest.

'Don't fight,' my father sighed.

'It's how it's done here, Joanne,' Laura said.

'This is my mother's funeral, and I will honour her the way I want to.'

'Please don't fight,' my father tried again.

'This is not the time for your feminist bullshit,' Laura bit. 'We'll do it the traditional way.'

'I'll do it the way I want to.'

'Girls, please…' my dad mumbled weakly.

Dad and Carolyn asked to see her body one last time.

I wasn't sure I could endure it, but I followed them into the room where the coffin lay. Someone pulled back the sheet. I ventured closer and forced myself to touch my mother's face.

But I wasn't prepared. The poet Jack Gilbert writes that the mouth is the porch of the body, the 'forecourt of the heart.' We kiss, he says, in our final moments because the mouth is 'close up against the spirit.' A kiss is 'the frontier' in us.

I could not kiss her in that coffin. Until you have touched the face of a person you love in which the fire has gone out, it is impossible to understand how the swish of blood and beat of a heart makes a person human. When the machine stops, there is no silence like it.

That frozen body was not my mother. She had left.

My sisters and I were taken into a small side room. My cousin came in with a razor blade and ritually made a cut into each of our shirts.

When we emerged, I glimpsed a few familiar faces in the throng. Theo. Zed's friends. How do people find out about funerals so quickly? It was confounding.

The coffin was wheeled out, and then we walked and walked, arm in arm, up and up and up the interminable hill. When we finally reached the site, we gathered around the grave, and the rabbi began.

And now his beard. His bloody beard.

I remove my mask to translate for Carolyn who cannot lipread through the foliage of the Rabbi's moustache. My mother was not a fan of rabbis, but of all of them, he was the one she disliked the least. He says all the right things, well prompted by my father. When the time comes, and all the men have scooped their three shovels of earth into the pit, I step forward to do the same. My sisters follow.

My father recites Kaddish, and the rabbi says, 'That concludes...'

But no, that does not conclude anything. I cut straight across him and begin to recite the Hebrew prayer for mourners, '*Yitkadal ve-yitkadash....*' And I hear my voice rise and sing and stifle the senselessness of excluding daughters from uttering their blessings when they lose a parent. I am my mother's daughter, and even though she was someone you could easily overlook, she was not to be trifled with. She could tell people to fuck off when it was time for them to fuck off, and right now, I am telling every man who ever thought it was okay to tell a woman how to behave, not to get in my way. I will say the prayer for my dead mother.

As I do, I hear my sister Laura joining in and we say the prayer together.

His moustache cannot conceal the Rabbi's displeasure.

No-one responds with 'Amen.'

When the crowd begins to disperse, Theo and Laurence, another friend of my mother's, thank me. They say we have set a precedent for their daughters to recite Kaddish for them.

We return to the house to too much food that has just appeared—sesame bagels, hard-boiled eggs, cinnamon babkas and apple cakes. We are all stunned into strangeness, even around food. Appetite seems inappropriate, vulgar almost.

Later the house fills with people for prayers, and instead of being grateful for the effort everyone has made, I am suffocated by their presence. I read out a message from Zed, who says my mother defied all stereotypes of the typical mother-in-law. He loved that she poured a heavy gin. His only complaint is how she used to supervise the *boerewors* barbequing. 'The only time I was ever scared of you was when you were shaking salt on your plate.'

Everyone laughs. I miss his humour. Right now, all I want is to be held by him.

Then I read a message from Jess: 'Your name 'is one of the first I remember,' 'buried deep in the most fundamental of my memories, times that built the foundations of me. I'm glad that the last moment we shared was full of music. I'm glad you left us in dreams. And I am going to miss you. Now this distance is untraversable, I love you, my nana.'

As soon as I can, I escape the mourning house, and alone in my Airbnb, on a strange bed overlooking the skyline of Johannesburg, I read Jess's letter *In Case of Emergency*. She reminds me that 'love knows no country lines or flight times…' and to 'let it be.'

The day after her funeral, I stand at my mother's wardrobe, reluctant to invade her privacy. I don't know what constitutes a respectable time after death, before we touch others' personal belongings. I work through each shelf, tentatively. I don't know what I'm looking for—perhaps something of hers I can take home that I could wear. I struggle to find anything. I settle on a nightie, a white beanie and a black t-shirt.

It is not unusual in South Africa, but on this day, the timing is uncanny. The gate buzzes, and a destitute man is there, begging for something to eat and clothes for his wife. I ask Dad if I can give some of mom's stuff away, and he says, 'yes, a few things,' and I put a bag together and take it to the man at the gate, who bows his head in thanks.

Then the visitors start. One of Dad's childhood friends sits and holds his hand for an hour, crying while Dad consoles him. My mother's closest friend, Angela, arrives with fried fish and chips for lunch. One after the other, a steady stream of people appears—all bearing food. By the end of the day, the kitchen is stacked, and I can barely talk.

Where is my mother to tell everyone to fuck off now? The loss suddenly feels dementing.

On her bed, Smudge sits, as if waiting for her to come back. Carolyn pays special attention to her, telling her that mom has gone, but she will look after her. See, Carolyn understands cats.

The house fills again for a second night of prayers, but I simply can't do another round. I stay upstairs on the bed with Smudge. I know I am being rude, just like my mother could be. It was a trait I once decided I disliked in her, so much so that I formed my personality to overcompensate. I tend to default into over-friendliness. Not tonight.

I feel now the quiet personal relief, the muscularity of expressing exactly how one feels, the freedom of not always adjusting to others' demands and needs. I want everyone to leave so I can leave. Later, I sob, unable to curb my distress. Dad unfurls his hand and says, 'Just let it go.'

He is so much stronger than I thought he'd be. With my mother gone, his anxiety about her going is tempered. His worst fear has been realised, and he is unbroken, softened by relief that she is no longer suffering. Looking at pictures of her from the past few weeks after the chemo, I see only pain etched on her face. That is all over now.

But when I crawl into bed in the Airbnb, in a room on the seventeenth floor, with a view of Johannesburg, the thought of Dad getting into bed alone guts me.

I wonder how long he will endure this life without her by his side. He has voiced it—that he hopes not for long. *Bring on the bananas.*

The next day I am lying on my mother's bed upstairs with Smudge. Nomusa comes in and asks, 'Are you still crying? You must stop now or you will get sick.'

It's been all of two days. But I smile. My mother would not want me to be this distressed. When I was nineteen, and my first boyfriend broke my heart, I spent two days sobbing in my bedroom; then she came in, opened the curtains and windows and told me, 'It's enough already.'

'I am so lucky I was here when she died,' I say.

Nomusa looks at me softly and says, 'God loves you, Joanne.' I close my eyes to receive the blessing of her words.

Sometimes the miracle we ask for is not the one we get.

People come and go in a constant stream for the whole week of *Shiva*. It is relentless and overwhelming. The food needs constant management, and it's what I occupy myself with. We are drowning in good deeds and bulkas, cakes and bagels. Cold meats and muffins. Everyone has put on weight.

My father easily handles being the centre of attention. He tells and retells his stories to every 'Tom, Dick and Harry,' as my mother would have said. He is an outstanding mourner, glad for the many visitors.

My mother couldn't bear the burdens of unfiltered company. She was a gatekeeper, a threshold guardian. One of Dad's friends once said she scared him. If Dad had gone first, she would have found the onslaught of the comforters intolerable. In this respect, she would have been a terrible widow.

Aidan calls to tell me he has gone through the recipe book we made for my mother's 80th birthday and put Post-it notes on all the recipes he wants to try. This gift to my mother has now returned to the commons and belongs to us all. I think my mother would be happy to live on in spaghetti bolognaise and mock crayfish.

As a family, we agree to fast-forward the unveiling of the tombstone, a ritual usually only carried out a year after someone dies, so that I can be here for it. Once I return to Australia, who knows when I'll be able to return.

It is up to me to organise it. I call on Lewis, one of my dearest and oldest friends, an architect who now lives in The Hague. There are dozens of decisions to be made—he sends me options for the colour of granite, the wording and the font. Do we want Hebrew text, candlesticks (as is common for Jewish women), stones or a slab? My head feels too ruptured to make sensible choices. I ask Lewis to guide me.

I gather everyone around the lunch table, and as a family we finally settle on the wording that is as concise and unwordy as my mother was: 'Nana: the anchor of our family.'

CHAPTER 19

I find two diaries hidden away in cupboards.

The sight of my mother's familiar handwriting causes a spasm in my throat, like aftershocks, the pangs that shake through me every time I remember she has died. It is, oddly, easy to forget.

I am not certain we are meant to read the deepest torments and confessions of our parents. Dying strips us of all our secrets. Beyond the physical invasions of resuscitation and preparation for burial, there are the raids on one's personality and history. People ferret through our drawers, examine our belongings, read our letters and uncover the things we hid away—maybe ones we even forgot about.

Still, I can't stop myself from reading my mother's. I hope there is a way of asking for forgiveness for this trespass.

One, written when she was sixteen, is filled with her musings about all the boys she's got crushes on and agonising about whether she is pretty enough. In the other, started when Jess was born, she forensically records everything her granddaughter uttered, all her new words and behaviours. She writes that this child is 'the light of her life' and that theirs is 'the most special connection.' When we moved to Cape Town she writes, 'now my darling girl will grow up far away from me,' and that she is 'torn asunder.'

'I'm so sorry, mom, I'm so sorry,' I howl. I realise only now that she did not recover. I never saw her happy again, not really. This journal is a record of personal anguish and sequestered grief. *We did that to her.* My heart flinches as the realisation lands: *we also did it to Jess.*

Zed was right—my mother had sad eyes after we left for Cape Town and I didn't see that. We were moving on with our lives, and we wrecked her heart in the process. She never let us know what a wrench it was for her. She kept it all secreted inside herself, and in these pages. *Oh Mama*. I pack the diary in my suitcase to give to Jess.

Later, Carolyn shows me another diary she found written when my mother was struggling to come to terms with having a deaf child. These are hard words for Carolyn to read, even as she is now the living proof of my mother's deepest hopes.

I realise that at devastating times in her life, my mother put words on the page. It's a part of her I never saw. She had a secret self.

I begin to wonder what else I never knew about her.

The executor arrives for Dad to sign the new will. It is surreal to see him just eight days after we saw him last, to discuss the finances with my mother in the room. He is professional; death is part of what he does. How does a person get used to it?

That night, Carolyn gives me a sleeping pill. All I want now is a decent night's sleep. I see how this can become a hunger, an anxiety, something that starts to elude you the more you crave it.

In the days that follow, I am dazed, almost concussed. My mother is gone. I tell myself this over and over again, like it's something I need to memorise, a teaching that must be retaught, recited; lines I must learn by heart, each telling etching it deeper until it becomes a groove, a smoothness that doesn't make me bleed every time I brush past it. Here in South Africa, I am untethered; bits of me are scattered everywhere, mostly, in the boot of my mother's car which I've been driving since my arrival. My longing is to be home with Zed and Archie, surrounded by my own things; my Coogee beach within reach becomes a savage thirst.

We have the saddest little Shabbat meal with the food Angela brings—chicken soup, chopped herring, chopped liver and *kichel*.

It is early days for furniture reshuffling, and it feels almost indecent, but Dad asks me to empty the bookshelf next to mom's bed and put it behind his desk in his study. I am clearing it when Carolyn walks in.

'What are you doing?' she berates me. 'Don't move things around. We need to keep everything left as it is.'

I tell her to calm down. I'm just doing what Dad asked.

Right now, we are a circus of misunderstandings; everyone's emotions are spiking and plummeting. None of us knows what we want or what the right moves are. We're all just fumbling around, trying to make order from this chaos. Grief is borne so individually.

We find five hairdryers in the cupboard amidst many unopened and unused items. Perfumes. Cosmetics. We discover what our mother kept, hoarded, held onto, never opened (waiting for that rainy day). We are learning so much about her, only now.

Carolyn empties the drawer next to her bed. I watch her pull out thermometers, pens, scissors, playing cards, lip balm. The spaces she filled are being unearthed and pillaged. But what else are we to do with someone else's clutter?

My father looks small and shrunken in his chair, unshaven. It's a *Shiva* thing. My mother would have hated it. He keeps repeating how relieved he is. Yes, it is a relief. But we are still in shock. He seems to be withering more every day as if it was her presence that gave him heft and bulk. Next to her, he seemed large. Now he is little. It is new to see him so retracted.

Then, tensions spark among us. A fight erupts. Everyone is shouting. Past hurts are hurled. *Why did you…? Why did you never…? Why were you always…?*

With my mother not here to stop us, things that were waiting to be expressed are shouted. She was the guardian, the protector, and without her as a silent watchdog, imploring us 'not to fight', holding us all in place, the wild things have escaped. The ground is shifting under our feet. It is strangely electrifying and destabilising.

Amid the shouting, I busy myself with getting lunch ready. I call everyone to the table, knowing food is where we can begin to soften and remember how to be the people we are capable of being. I know if she were here, mom would have cut a swathe through it all, with one caustic, 'I don't need all this shit, can we talk about something else?' She would hate that we are fighting. She always avoided conflict. This was her shadow as much as her light.

I finally get everyone to the table. I ladle soup into bowls. We eat bread.

Over lunch, painful history is aired. This one apologises, that one accepts the apology. Misunderstandings unravel. People say, *I love you.* It's as if a cork has popped. I feel the gentle ripple of understanding seeping in. Everyone stops holding on so tightly to their positions. Who is right and who is wrong evaporates. Everything eases.

Mother exits, and Act 1 is over. We can let go of the personas we all played in that configuration. The roles my mother played now fall to us. Suddenly, we understand that we all need each other more than ever.

I am led through the back entrance so I can enter the stage without having to meet and greet any parents. The casual chit-chat of social etiquette is beyond me right now. I have to get through the next fifteen minutes, that is all. I was promised I could speak first, deliver my valedictory address and get the hell out of there before anyone can congratulate me or worse, wish me long life.

I couldn't pull out just two days before and leave them without a guest speaker. Or maybe I could have. I don't know. This is the first time I've lost a mother.

My hair looks good, though. Earlier in the day, I'd taken myself to a hairdresser. As I'd lain with my head in the warm hands of a woman called Cecelia, it fell out of me. *My mother passed away last week.* The news is impossible to keep to myself.

'I know this pain, I know this pain,' Cecelia repeated, even though she lost her mother many years ago. I wondered then, does it never leave?

Later, Jocelyn, a friend from school days, picks me up and drives me to the school. When we are parked, she hauls out a bottle of whiskey and two shot glasses.

'Maybe after,' I say.

I haven't prepared a proper speech—just a few notes I managed to scribble before my mother died. I stand up on stage, and for a moment, I feel as if I might have a panic attack. Everyone is seated two metres apart, in masks. It's a scene out of a science fiction movie. But I hold steady. *Be cool*, I hear my mother saying. I try not to catch anyone's eye. I feel bruisable, as if the slightest touch will cause me terrible harm, like someone with that neurological condition, allodynia.

Somehow, I get through it.

Back in the car, Jocelyn pulls out the whiskey again. This time, I take a searing slug.

CHAPTER 20

My friend Ilze drives me straight from the Cape Town airport to the ocean. I'd booked this trip when my mother was alive, thinking I could slink away for ten days between her chemo sessions. After she died, I was going to cancel it, but Dad encouraged me to go. 'You need the break,' he'd said.

Whenever I have flown to Cape Town, a detour I've made every trip to South Africa, I have always felt guilty spending time away from my mother. I could always sense her impatience and disappointment when I'd leave, and her agitation for me to get back to Johannesburg. Time with Ilze has always meant time away from her. Now, I am released from that contest. My father doesn't need me in the same way she did.

I begin to wonder, long-term, what other liberties her death will yield.

In the car, I change into my bathing suit, goggles and cap and with my perfectly blow-dried hair, I sink into the water at the Dalebrook pool, and Ilze joins me for her first swim of the season. I let the waves rumble and lap at me. I only want to be sodden, loved once more by tiny fish, seaweed and salt. I flip around like a sealion. And I swim and I swim and I swim.

Here, in Muizenberg, I am returned to a different self in the comfort of this decades-old friendship. We eat fish and chips together at Kalk Bay. Tucked in a single bed in Ilze's study, with the peak of Silvermine mountain peeking through the window, surrounded by her books, I have a truly good night's sleep.

I awake to the news that there is no more hotel quarantine for travellers returning to NSW—not even isolation. I will be able to swim as soon as I return and resume my life when I land. I feel as if I've just received a pardon from a long sentence.

In the Sisters WhatsApp group, Carolyn tells us that the oncologist wept when she spoke to her, shocked at mom's death that she speculates was caused by a pulmonary embolism. We wonder together about mom's last night. Did she sense the end was coming? Did she call Bridget to help her empty her bladder in preparation?

We all want answers… we have none, we can only guess and surmise and imagine.

During the week, Carolyn texts to say she has just picked up the death certificate and is lying on the floor in her office with the door closed, sobbing. There is no way I know to console her. The sadness is seeping in as everyone tries to understand the shape my mother's leaving has left behind. The loss has new depths we keep discovering. They appear, without warning, like the circumstances of an accident.

One morning, Ilze drives me to Simonstown to Water's Edge beach so I can swim freely in open water, beyond the walls of an ocean bath. There, I dive deep for an abalone shell, and swim amongst the kelp forests. The ocean here is different to the water in Coogee, thicker, more viscous and saltier, perhaps from the kelp. Places have their own signature waters, like they do skies. The African sky is not the same sky as the one in the outback. Highveld thunderstorms are their own thing entirely, unlike any other.

With penguins plopping in and scrambling out from the surrounding rocks, the salt in every orifice and crevice, I am part of this deep, dark blue water. I have always found it hard to get out of the ocean, and now, more so than ever. It's like forcing myself to wake from a perfect dream.

One morning I wake early and make my way down to Muizenberg beach. I am from these waters. They run in my family's lineage. We have swum here for generations.

I walk on the hard sand down the long stretch of beach. There is hardly a soul about, just the seagulls and a few scattered shells. Here, parts of me that are folded when I'm with my family, balloon and expand, like wings, a parachute. I remember entire landscapes of who I am, beyond being a daughter and sister.

I feel strangely light, improperly so. I have gone through whole days where I don't think about the fact that my mother has just died. How is that possible? As the breaking waves wet my feet, I try to feel into the true pain of what it means to have lost her, but in this moment, I can't. It feels wrong not to be falling apart. I am upended; I know this rationally. But I can't feel it. I don't know if I am okay or not. Where is the map of this territory so I know where I am in this journey of grief?

Maybe it's because I know what it feels like to miss my mother. I have missed her for twenty years from afar. I have needed my mama so often and had to survive without her. I have developed calluses in my needy places. The ache of separation has always been softened by the promise that we'd be together again in the future. But that has changed. *We will never see each other again.* I feel myself getting stuck on this impossible thought. Folded into that 'never again' are many other 'never agains'—never again will we all be together as a family, around her Shabbat table. Never again will she cook *kneidlach* or make chopped herring. Never again will I call her to tell her the inanities of my day, never again will I say goodbye to her. All that has gone with her going.

The peace of the past few days feels tenuous, and I begin to sense a nervous dread, like I'm waiting to feel an enormity of emotion, terrified of it overtaking me, consuming me, wondering when it will strike.

I stand and look back along the sweep of this majestic shoreline.

We loved each other.

Everything between us was complete.

God loves you, Joanne.

Yes, this is what it feels like to be loved. To be in the right place at the right time when it matters.

I see a couple of grey-haired surfers emerging from the waves, perhaps a man and wife. They are filled with the delight of the early morning sea, and the adrenaline of surfboard adventures. Everything about them tells a tale, the antithesis of my mother's fearful existence in which she tried to keep us safe at all costs, with reminders never to walk barefoot, in case we stood on glass, or to swim after eating, in case we got a cramp. As afraid as I have been of life at times, my mother was petrified.

My mother's anxiety has shaped my life—even from before I was born. I had no agency to claim a birthday but was assigned one by a medical procedure just so her worry could be assuaged, that I was 'normal.' Now that she is gone, the energetic fetter of her apprehension has slackened. Her death has changed the point of view of my story.

I can feel myself on the Lazy Susan of sorrow, slowly turning to look back over my life and my choices and wondering if I have lived an avoidant, risk-averse life, just to protect her.

When I was a child, my mother brought me and my sisters to swim at the St James Ocean Bath. I remember a holiday we spent close to this little rockpool. On my final morning in Cape Town, I dive into the icy water in front of the coloured wooden booths at the beach.

As I pull my hands through the water, I try to sense where my mother's spirit went. Did it become diluted into the everything? And if so, how will I ever find her again? I don't even know what I'm looking for.

As my fingers start to pucker, reminding me I have been in the sea a while, it wallops me, the sense that I am at the beginning of something immense, and my anguish is just waiting for me. I have a long, long way to go. I am terrified of what will happen when it catches up with me.

I search the pool bed and finally settle on a rock the size of an ostrich egg, which I will pack in my luggage and take back to Johannesburg. I know exactly where I am going to place it.

The first draft Lewis sends me of the tombstone has my mother's name incorrectly spelled: DOREEN instead of DORRINE. And he's left off 'Nana.' He keeps suggesting more embellishments. I remind him to keep it modest and simple, as she was. I finally settle on the cheapest stone because I know she'd want her money to be for the living. My mother was practical like that.

Tending to the gravesite, he reminds me, is the last *mitzvah* we perform, the last rite we undertake, one that has no quid pro quo. It is done purely to honour the person we loved. He invites me to come stay with him and his wife in the Hague before I fly back to Australia. 'Just extend your trip, you're already halfway here,' he says.

I can't… I think. But then it strikes me my refusal is tied to the thought that I cannot leave my mother. A new sense of autonomy flares inside me.

I tell him I'll think about it.

CHAPTER 21

My father has had to have all his pants taken in. Over the past fortnight he's lost so much weight that they were falling off him. Back in Johannesburg, I watch him sink into being alone. It is a terrible new reality to navigate. The house is filled with confectionery—everyone has brought cheesecake and baklava and apple strudel, as if all that sugar could fill the emptiness and sweeten the darkness.

'You look tired,' my father says. 'You must be homesick; it's been so hard for you,'

I don't tell him the truth—that I wish this trip was over. I just want to feel the deep rest of being back in my life in Sydney.

My mother's bed is now taken over by his stuff, the way I spread out in our king-sized bed when Zed goes away for a weekend. At her dressing table, where I used to preen as a kid and teenager, I help myself to her makeup, perfumes and creams. I try on all her lipsticks. None of them suits me.

I fold the clothes in her wardrobe. Some items are full of dust, others just collapse, the elastic finally giving up its stretch. I find a pink scarf, the bandanas I bought her when she was having chemo, unopened and unused, and a sweatshirt I might keep. She had grace and beauty, but as she aged, comfort always won out over fashion, and she thought nothing of wearing trainers to a wedding or a bar*mitzvah* so her feet didn't get cold. For a time, as a young woman, she'd dressed as a hippie in glorious golden kaftans. I am filled with curiosity about her choices and what they reveal about her as a person. Aren't we all, in the end, weirdos to everyone but ourselves?

Carolyn has cleared away so much clutter that Dad complains he doesn't know where anything is.

Alone with Dad one afternoon, we default into watching TV. I suggest *Maid*, which I've heard has good reviews. Two episodes in, it's a disastrous choice. He asks me to switch it off.

'The house suddenly feels too big,' he sighs.

We sit and hold hands and cry together. When Nomusa comes in to prepare his dinner, she looks at our faces and asks us what's wrong. I tell her we've been watching a programme about a woman who runs away from a man who beats her.

She shakes her head and clicks her tongue. 'Don't watch this one,' she berates, with her hands on her hips.

Dad laughs. She is a balm in this sad house.

I pour my father a whiskey and take him outside to sit in the garden as the evening ventures in, where the light and flowers and jacarandas might lift his spirit. But the truth is, we are fighting deep panic. A monstrous loss crouches at the base of everything, the way your stomach can feel like it's falling, as we remember: she is gone. It's such a terrible thing for her not to be here.

Dad tells me about a song called 'Gloomy Sunday,' written in 1933 by a struggling Hungarian Jewish composer, Rezso Seress, which was banned because it was said to have caused people to commit suicide. It used to depress him as a child with its lyrics 'Love has died on earth… the world has ended, hope has ended.'

'It's Gloomy Sunday from hereon in,' he sighs.

I squeeze his hand.

I water the garden.

I lead him back indoors to his comfortable chair.

I start the grandfather clock.

I change the water in all the vases.

I ask him about his death directive, what does he want for himself, when he gets near his own end?

'No resuscitation,' he is adamant.

I need that on record, so I put my phone recorder on and he repeats, 'No resuscitation.'

'And I don't want to go back to hospital.'

'Who does, Dad?'

'I also don't want to be in pain—bring on the morphine.'

'And what music would you want played if Jewish funerals allowed?'

'Beethoven's Seventh, the third movement,' he says.

I find it on Spotify and play it for him, and he holds his head and weeps.

'It cuts right through me.'

I am learning about my father now too. I wonder what my mother would have asked for. Maybe 'Hallelujah'.

He says he had prayed for a blessing for her and realises now that the way she went, and how quickly she went, was, in fact, the only possible blessing.

He keeps thinking about the state of her body and at what point of decomposition it is. Is that morbid? I don't know. I remember how he stood over her corpse in the bed and looked into her face, searching it, etching it into his mind's eye. How he wanted to look at her face again when the men brought her down, wrapped in black plastic. And again, at the funeral, before we buried her. Just one more look. Maybe that's what artists do—they look at things as they are to see what is in front of them.

Dad talks about her beauty.

'The most beautiful woman I'd ever seen,' he says.

He tells me that he knew it was his destiny to lose his wife and to have to survive that loss. I wonder if this is an echo of his mother's 'it's no good' that he's carried all his life. As we sit together and survey this landscape, I am starting to get a sense of how this game works. Those first three weeks of relief and gratitude that she was out of suffering were a con, a false positive. Now all that's left is a never-going-away emptiness. My head instructs me, Mom is dead, you will never see her again, and my heart says FUCK YOU. *No. I don't believe you. Prove it.* But even with all the evidence, my brain, as if it's padlocked and bolted down, won't allow the information in.

My father falls on his face rushing to get to the gate to open it. It is his second fall in a few days. He philosophises that he's been spiralling downwards and that he had to fall to feel the pain. He is a black and blue catastrophe in an armchair.

Every day is now a monstrous effort. My sisters work during the week, so I keep Dad company. *Shiva* is over, so I am his only company other than Nomusa. There is nowhere for me to turn but here.

One day, he says he feels 'lucky.' The next, he has no passion to live. He cannot help but broadcast his every emotional state as if it were a public service announcement. My mother was the firewall against his emotional onslaught. She held it all at bay. I wonder how she coped, and then I remember, she medicated him. In my strained moments, I wish I had a tranquilliser or an episode of *Jane the Virgin* to offer him. I remind myself to be careful not to get caught up in my father's grief.

Each night I pray she will visit me while I'm asleep, just so I can see her again. I do not understand why she has not come to me in my dreams. Isn't that where the dead wait for us?

I repot geraniums in the window boxes, so they overflow with flowers and colour. The succulents I planted when I first arrived are doing well, throwing up their little tendrils of flowers.

Each day, for the few hours of South African loadshedding when the electricity is shut down to prevent a total national grid collapse, we sit in the dark together. I think of how my mother would have been fretting, endlessly checking the WhatsApp group for updates. She was never able to relax and just sit out the hours, trusting that the power would return. *Yes, but when?* She always wanted to know where she was, to stay in control.

The shadows from the afternoon skulk in and hover around us, as if this is a set in a play, and the stage directions call for symbolic correlatives of the mood that finds us where we are. *Centre stage, low lights. Father stooped. Daughter reaches for his hand. Long silences between them.*

I listen to my father's stories, letting him ramble on.

'I hate that painting,' my father says, squinting through the dim light at one of his own paintings of a man painting a scene in a field. It hangs above the TV.

'Your mother liked it,' he sighs.

Suddenly, we are bereft of all her quirks.

Like the way she would wedge the door of the downstairs toilet room open with a little dustbin. It's what we call in Yiddish, a *meshugas*, a madness. Dad declares he's not doing it anymore. The door to the toilet room will stay closed, he pronounces. He tells me he's enjoying not having to be in bed by 5 pm, which was my mother's preference, and the freedom from watching crap soap operas and *Come Dine with Me*. He gets to hold the remote control for the first time in his life.

He says he misses her nightly ritual of giving him a handful of gummy lollies. Then she'd ask, 'Do you want a bit of chocolate?' and give him half a Snickers bar. He relays that now, each night as he gets into bed, he gives himself a handful of gummy lollies and half a Snickers bar. We sit with this tenderness between us for a few moments.

'But it's not the chocolate I miss. It's her giving me half the chocolate.' And right inside that sentence, curled like the most tender of innermost fronds, is the deepest understanding between two people intricately bound by the smallest gestures over a lifetime.

This Sunday has arrived to teach us what meaningless and empty truly is. The space she leaves on the sofa. The untouched pots and pans in the kitchen, the emptying fridge, freezer and pantry. This is what every suggestion of loneliness in all our lifetimes ever promised—that someday, we will come to know what un-fake heartache is; anguish without performance or agenda. It has arrived. She brought it. I know she'd be sorry to have been the one to evoke these emotions. But she was selected to be 'it.' The bearer of sorrow.

'I don't see the point of living anymore now that she is gone. No-one needs me,' my father says.

'Dad, we need you,' I say softly. 'When you die, we won't only lose you, we'll lose her all over again.'

How instantly a life and its habits can change. My father lies quietly on the couch, a bag of skin and bones, eyes closed. He has pressure sores, a beard, bad sciatica and can't bear the noise of the television. He puts on the movies he wants to watch. None of the inane shows my mother loved. But with all that autonomy, he doesn't see the point in anything—in food, swimming, watching TV. These all had meaning through and because he shared them with someone he loved. I watch him chew a mouthful of muffin for fifteen minutes without being able to swallow it. He is disappearing, but not fast enough for himself.

'What shall we do?'

'We carry on,' Dad says.

What does 'on' mean? I ask.

'I wish I could find the off switch,' he says.

I suggest we have White Russians, the cocktail from *The Big Lebowski*, our favourite Coen Brothers movie. I pour us a pair of drinks, mixing vodka, Kahlua and milk in long glasses which jostle with ice cubes.

As I hand my dad his glass, I say, 'Hey careful man, there's a beverage here,' quoting a line from the movie where the dude is being wrestled into a car and trying not to spill his drink.

And my father chuckles.

I finally finish watching the hundredth episode of *Jane the Virgin*. I am sad it is over. There are so many questions I wish I could have discussed with my mother. They sit inside me, unhatched. Did she like

Michael or Raphael better? What did she think of Jane? What was her favourite moment? I feel how my loss is wound up in this story, and how, through my darkest hours, Jane walked by my side.

It is no small joy to discover that Bridget, who relieves Nomusa every second weekend and stays over with my father, is the same shoe size as my mother. We give her most of mom's shoes.

Bridget is overcome—she has never had so many pairs of trainers, slippers and Crocs. She says she 'only knew Madam for two days.' It's as if she's asking whether it's okay to take all these possessions. She met my mother on a Friday afternoon and was doing chest compressions on Sunday morning. We reassure her that there is no-one else we'd rather have them.

She also takes all my mother's DD-sized bras, though they don't fit her. She says she will take them to her church and hand them out. We give her all the vests too—my mother had a thing for them, to keep the cold at bay. Bridget is filled with exuberance at the abundance, already imagining the reception she will get on Sunday when she arrives with a bushel of supportive undergarments. Her delight is a solace in this ransacked house.

As we leave after the Friday night meal, Laura turns to Bridget and says, 'Let's hope nobody dies this weekend.'

I laugh so hard I wet myself. I carry on laughing when I get in my car, and then the laughing turns to crying.

There is one who utters the outrageous.

The one who laughs.

And the one who disapproves. Carolyn does not find it funny.

It is impossible to know what is funny anymore.

CHAPTER 22

My old friend Lewis is at the Amsterdam airport waiting for me with a bunch of flowers. It's been many years since I've seen him in person, but he is my kin, a man I once dated in my early twenties, beloved by my parents and sisters. The past that holds us is vast and I am folded into the ease of being with him.

On the flight from Johannesburg, I had a peculiar sense of flying in the wrong direction, as if I was being carried further away from Zed and the kids and Coogee. It was as if my internal compass, which has always been set to 60 The Braids Road, had been tampered with and the settings readjusted. Where is 'away' now? And what is 'coming back'? My mother was the force, the magnet that always pulled me. When she was here, I knew where I was. It was always in relation to where she was.

I ask Lewis to drive me straight to the ocean. There aren't many places to swim in Scheveningen in the Hague, but he finds me a spot where locals dunk, edged by a stone pier. I am blasted by the cold water. My skin burns and numbs, but I need the shock. Lewis tries to get in with me, but it's bloody freezing, and he calls me crazy, and if you knew Lewis, you'd make a sentence with the words 'pot', 'kettle' and 'black.'

We walk along the dock with all the fish shops with their resplendent array of herring, cod and mackerel. We eat raw 'haring' (herring) smothered in chopped onion like you would a fast-food hot dog. It is the creamiest, smoothest, most delicious snack. My god, it takes herring to a new place. But who will I tell? Besides my mother, no-one gets excited about herring. Zed's indifference, verging on antipathy to this fish, is a scab of contention in our relationship.

I am comforted by being with someone I have known for thirty-three years, someone who knew and loved my mother. I let myself flop into Lewis' plans which include his adamance that I must see Paris. I have never been, and we are so close, just a short train ride away.

We are up at 5 am, running for the tram in the dark, onto a train to Rotterdam and finally on the Thalys to Paris. We dash around the city on scooters. Lewis takes me to the Jewish Quarter, to a bakery where he buys poppyseed cake, almond cigars and cheesecake. I buy a red beret with a silver spiral I will probably never wear again, and black leather walking shoes in a shop for women with big feet. Europe is everything I long for with its cobbled streets and little shops and markets and places where people sit and drink coffees and walk along rivers.

Back at our hotel, Lewis gets into an ugly fight with the manager Christof, about our tiny rooms because they're meagre little cupboards with no windows and not what he booked for us. He is adamant that my first time in Paris must be memorable. Christof is adamant that there are no other rooms available. Lewis should come with a warning—he has stamina and can hang on, way past anyone else's breaking point. It is one of his superpowers. Then, mid-argument, his phone rings. He answers loudly, in Yiddish. Suddenly, Christof grabs hold of his hand, crying, because he too, is a Jew and here, in a dark Parisian reception area, he belts out a Hebrew Sabbath song, '*le-cha dodi likrat kalah...*' and Lewis, never one to miss a cue, sings along. This is the sort of wild shit that happens when you hang around with him.

Christof finds better rooms for us, mine even has a balcony overlooking the city.

This lunacy makes us a bit manic and hysterical. I laugh and cry at the same time.

'I love Lewis,' my mother always said.

That afternoon, in front of the Eiffel Tower, I exhale. 'Finally, here I am,' but I'm sideswiped by the realisation that my mother never got to see it. I walk into the Opera House, searching for the ceiling Chagall painted. It makes me want to kneel and kiss the earth. All these encounters start to back up, and I feel a sense of strange panic. Never have I accumulated so many new experiences, without relaying them to my mother, who always wanted to know every detail, mostly 'what did you eat?' All my joy comes up against a wall and bounces back at me, with nowhere to land. Why can't I just enjoy experiences for me? Has my life always been an arrangement of vicarious exchange with her?

Over lunch, my phone pings. It is an email from the Rabbi with images of my mother's gravestone. There is her name, carved in stone. At the place we laid her body to rest. I gasp. *Oh my god, my mother died*, I remember for the thousandth time.

Lewis, who lost both his parents many years ago, just sits with me as the tears fall into my cappuccino.

In Amsterdam, I get into a fight with one of the officials at the Anne Frank House who demands my passport, Covid vaccine certificates, as well as a PCR test *from today*.

'Today?' I ask. 'I've had no problems getting into other museums with this,' I flap my frayed certificate at him.

'It's technically not enough. You need a PCR test every day while you're travelling overseas.'

'Dear God, are you hearing yourself?' I yell at him through the stifle of my facemask, 'How ridiculous and unreasonable this is?' I heap my pent-up rage about everything onto this hapless official. He eventually relents, and I wander furiously through the tiny rooms in which Anne and her family hid until they were betrayed by neighbours.

I remember the story of the 'Tainted Grain', one of Rebbe Nachman of Breslov's tales, the mystic storyteller and philosopher who used creative parables to teach spiritual truths. In this story, the king's stargazer informed him that the grain for the coming season was tainted and anyone who ate of it would go mad. He suggested that he and the king set aside a small amount of the untainted grain so that the two of them might keep their sanity. But the king refused, saying that they should eat of the tainted grain too, go mad with the rest of the population, but place a mark on each other's foreheads so that whenever he and the stargazer looked at each other, they would remember that they were mad.

I sometimes think these facemasks are just that mark.

Eventually fatigue takes hold of me. These twelve weeks feel like bags of sand I am lugging around. I am depleted and tearful.

I calculate that I have changed beds eighteen times since my arrival. I have lived in the limbo of jumbled suitcases and car boots and new beds for three months, without the truce of sinking my head into a pillow with which it has a history of dreams. Finally, all a person wants to do is stop. To lie down in a familiar place and rest. I have tired of it all—the travelling, family, friends… I have come to the end of my desire to be away from my little uneventful life in Coogee, and I yearn for its simplicity and quietness. I long to pull back the covers of my own bed, slip in and wait for Archie to come find the curve of my arm into which he fits as if he were designed to slot in, and to reach out for Zed in the night. I am made of thousands of such nights; they are braided in me like nerves, and all I wish for is to wake up for sunrise and a swim in my ocean. When it's all stripped away, the heart simply pines for the repeat of what it knows and trusts.

I have my can't-remember-what-number Covid PCR test for my flight back to Johannesburg, dole out the extravagant fee yet again, and realise with elation, only one more nurse in a Hazmat suit will poke a stick up my nose before I am homeward bound.

Flying back to Johannesburg without my mother waiting there for me is a confusing feeling of home-not-home. My heart stutters, unable to form the language of where I am now.

CHAPTER 23

My fingernails are dirty, my palms and knees, brown. I refused the garden gloves. I want to be marked with this soil.

Two young men preparing a nearby gravesite watch on, silent witnesses to four women lifting heavy bags. Nomusa is helping me and my sisters cover the burial site with pink stones and pebbles. This is a humble undertaking usually left to those paid to do the job. It is physical *watch your back, bend your knees, careful, do you need help?* labour. We move around the little plot silently, sweating and toiling, each daughter quiet in her own thoughts. The day is cool, and we are all wearing jumpers, socks and closed shoes. Now and then we stop to take a sip of water and look out at the view of the city from the plot where my mother is laid to rest. Some tasks are by their nature, righteous duties. If we outsource them, what we miss is not the act as much as what the act binds us to; in our case, the joint story of mine and my sisters' childhoods, family meals, holidays, shared jokes and heartbreaks—all because we were born to the same mother.

I place the St James rock in the centre, and Carolyn sprinkles Dad's stone collection from a lifetime of beach holidays around it.

Finally done, we stand back, arms linked and observe the manual labour of our hands. It is smiling work.

The preparation of the gravesite heralds my departure, and my dominant emotion is relief. I have six more sleeps. Poor sleep. Fair sleep. My Garmin sleep reports sound like Shakespearean addresses to sleep itself.

On the last Friday night dinner with my family, we light my mother's Shabbat candles and recite the blessing. We hold onto each other like we did at her funeral on the way up to the grave and stand staring into those flames, tears streaming, each of us lost inside our own skin as her absence fills us.

The dinner is stressful despite the feast we prepared of roast duck, stuffing, apple sauce, sweet and sour red cabbage—all our mother's recipes. Perhaps it is the full moon I notice on the way back to Carolyn's house that causes madness to erupt among us, or my impending departure, or grief settling bitingly, or fatigue or mom's absence becoming less obscure, or the fact that no food can fill the void of her being gone, or the reality of it all, or the anger that is grief's emissary, or how alone we each feel without her. It is a disaster; despite the hard work we all put into the dinner.

It dawns on me that not everything we touch in her honour, turns to magic.

On Sunday we are back at her gravesite for the unveiling of the tombstone. The wind whips at us from all sides. With the rose quartz chunks we have placed around the St James rock, in the shape of a flower, my mother's grave is beautiful. But there are not enough men to form a *minyan*, the traditional number needed for a Jewish quorum.

The main roads are closed for a bike race through Johannesburg. People are stuck in traffic. Our phones buzz in our pockets with apologies. We stand around in the blustery gale, and it takes as much restraint as I can muster not to blow this party up since we have more than enough people here—but women don't count by Jewish law. It was precisely this sort of inequity that left my mother cold when it came to religion. My father is struggling to stand, and I ask if we can proceed, nonetheless. But the orthodox among us will not start without the full kosher quotient, and a chair is summoned for my father while we wait it out. Laurence whispers that, 'Dorrine wouldn't have come to her own unveiling.' We chuckle, imagining her irritation. At last, a few latecomers straggle in, sweaty with apology, and finally, we're allowed to proceed. The blessings are recited, Dad says Kaddish and we, the three daughters, repeat it too. I help Carolyn through the English transliteration of the prayer. And then it is done.

I hold my niece Jenna tight and say goodbye in the cemetery parking lot. This is one of the hardest partings for me.

At Carolyn's house we have a final barbeque, in my mother's honour. The chops are delicious and the *boerewors* is not overcooked.

Around the table, I let it be known by announcement that I don't want anyone to lay their sadness about me going on me. I am saying goodbye to many—they are saying goodbye to one. I need everyone to be brave and sensible. I am not dying, I am just flying home, and I will speak to everyone in a few days. I cannot cope with histrionics at this moment. *Just be cool.* I hear my mother coming out in me.

Abysmal. The day before my departure, that's the word Dad uses to describe how he's feeling. He can't get out of bed. He doesn't know how to face the world. He is contrite about an argument we had the night before. I tell him I understand that we're all grieving, that we all lose our shit at times. As my departure looms, all the losses come flooding in and become cojoined and indistinguishable.

He says he feels confined to the house and wants to do a Freddy Mercury and 'break free'.

Now that my mother is not here, he's looking for a new patron on whom to offload his emotions. But I cannot do what my mother did.

'There will be days like this,' I say. 'You could go on for years.'

'Shh,' he warns, as if saying it might make it true.

Life, I see, can be too long, as much as it can be too short.

It is my last night in Carolyn's house.

My packed bags are filled with blankets my mother knitted, trinkets and talismans of her existence. I have managed to avoid accidents, hijackings, putting my back out and contracting Covid. I feel myself exhaling and my nervous system slowing down. Soon, I will be able to release the stresses of travelling, being a guest, foreign beds, poor bedside lighting, negotiating other peoples' spaces, fridges, routines and wondering where and when I'll swim. The enormous fatigue of these accumulations is starting to lift like a bad spell. The homecoming I have been longing for is almost within reach.

I have my final Covid test and log in to an Australian website to get authorisation to travel. When the big green tick appears on my screen, I burst into tears. I am really going home across the ocean to where my other family awaits. I will put my grief on hold until I get there and unpack this mystery of how my mother slipped sleeping into the silence of the night.

These three months were meant to be time with my mother. What a strange mockery of our intentions life turns out to be. I did not want to endure seven and a half weeks without her here. But—and this realisation slams into me—without Covid and the strict travel requirements of having to stay for three months, I would probably have come for a few weeks only, and the chances are, I would have missed her death.

Go now.

I caught the wave and it brought me here, to live this sorrow.

When I land back in Australia, I will have been gone for 98 days. It is long enough to become an entirely different person.

On my last morning, Carolyn makes us scrambled eggs, and we sit and hold hands in her kitchen.

At 60 The Braids Road, I swim the lengths of the pool for the last time and spill my tears in that chlorinated body of water. My leaving was always a brutal anguish for my mother. I realise I will never again have to break her heart by leaving her standing in the driveway of 60 The Braids Road, waving bravely, though her heart was torn asunder.

I weep when I say goodbye to Nomusa. I do not cry saying goodbye to Dad and my sisters.

My kids message me to say they're excited to see me soon and *travel safe mum.*

I tickle Smudge's stomach and note those flowers I pulled out on the concrete circle outside, thinking they were weeds, are flowering now, gorgeous and pink. They have come back and are blooming just as I am going home.

PART 4

GOING HOME

CHAPTER 24

After twenty-seven hours behind a facemask, eight movies and Jess's final letter *Flight Back*, I glimpse the ocean as we begin our descent. The Sydney coastline comes into full view through my window. I heave huge, ugly gulps behind my mask. Relief is almost its own kind of distress.

Jess's words, 'I hope you are returning full of the joy for time with Nana and gratitude for seeing that place that lives cradled in the nostalgic streets of my memory,' are from a time Before, from an innocence lost now, forever.

I am the first one off the plane. First through customs. First at the baggage carousel. Then we wait. And wait. The carousel doesn't move. Finally, an announcement: a thunderstorm. They cannot offload our bags until it passes. We were lucky to have landed just before it broke.

It's as if the universe is pulling at me, like a dog on a leash. The hour that passes is like its own mini-lockdown, and I can do nothing but chill out and text Aidan, who is waiting for me just beyond these walls, 'I'm sorry, bags still not out.'

Zed is not with him—he'd been offered the chance to be on a support team for a runner on a 240km race, and I'd encouraged him to go. We've been apart for so long, another few days won't matter. 'Go, go be in the mountains,' I'd said. My God, we all need the mountains, the oceans and the forests in the aftershocks of Covid.

At the stalled baggage carousel, I help a young mother with a newborn strapped to her chest and a manic toddler, find her missing pram, which is at a distant carousel, because arrival terminals in airports are not designed by mothers. I expend my frustration, raging at husbands who fly business class, leaving their wives to wipe up spit and manage tantrums, as we all wait out the storm.

After an hour, the bags finally start to come through—everyone's but mine. With only thirty minutes in Singapore to change flights, it's probably been left behind, and, at this point, I am past caring. I am spitting to get the hell out of here, to rip this mask from my face, and breathe. I just want to go home. Finally, an official asks for my baggage tag. As she does, my blue bag emerges from the maw of the baggage carousel like a baby's head after a lengthy labour, squashed and battered.

Aidan has been waiting so long, he doesn't see me walk through the gate, earphones in, face down in his phone. I have to call his name to get his attention, but there he is, my gorgeous boy. I lean against this huge man who is my child, hold him close, and I rest in this belonging.

He drives me home in the muggy late afternoon. I don't need talking, just this proximity. To be able to reach out and touch his arm, to know he is real, that my family back here wasn't just a dream. He takes me past Coogee beach. I am filled with wonder to see it again. It is real, it exists.

He pulls up outside our apartment. *Here, here is where I live.* I have played over in my mind the moment I would see Dolphin Street again, and walk up the few stairs to our home. All the plants are overgrown; it is a place that has been left to be its wild self. The Garden of Sanity my neighbour and I cobbled together during Covid is in disarray, overrun and chaotic. It wears my absence.

Suddenly I feel arms flung around me, and it is Jess, and we stand in the driveway hugging, crying. My child of The Six Letters.

I have been away so long, I have forgotten who loves me, what is mine and how I live.

I walk through the front door, a stranger in my own home, the carpet so soft underfoot. What a beautiful home. What rooms. What loveliness. I am overcome with the strangeness and familiarity of it all. I am meeting myself all over again, as if I had lived and died, and then returned to see what I chose to surround myself with. It's almost as surreal as rifling through my mother's things. Each item I find is an enchantment, a restoration. And there is Archie, unsure at first, but then brushing against my calf, and this right here is heaven.

The kids and their partners have prepared a Thai green curry for my homecoming. We sit around the kitchen table, me feeling like a guest in my own home, they, at ease using my pots and pans and utensils.

Zed has left a basket of loving goodies for me—a brand-new GoPro, and all my favourite foods; marinated artichokes, dried apricots, mint aero chocolate, Campos coffee, oat milk, pickled cucumbers, anchovy paste. With each item I touch, I remember, *he knows me*. I am known here. I unpack messily without having to stress the limits of his tolerance, and that too, is a relief. I can just be fully myself. I wander through the rooms, bewildered, having forgotten where I keep my valuables, my shoes, my this's and that's. I will have to rediscover it all again. I didn't think to make notes for myself before I left, not fully understanding that I would be someone different when I came back.

Jess lies in my arms on the couch and confesses how much she has missed me over the past fourteen weeks. She never told me she had to take a week off work and stay in bed after her Nana died—she hadn't wanted to burden me.

She has my mother in her, that restraint.

Jess stays the night with me. It is one of the few times it has been just the two of us, like the night she was born, and I cradled her in my arms, refusing to surrender her to the nursery so I could get a good night's sleep, which the nurses were pretty strict about, but I had been stricter. *Don't you dare take my child away.*

It is 4 am and pissing down with rain. I am awake after four hours of jetlagged sleep. I don't care what my Garmin says, it is rest in my own bed, and that is Good Sleep. I wait for 5 am and slip out to get a coffee at Chish and Fips, the beachfront kiosk, anticipating questions about my whereabouts—but no-one asks where I have been for the past three months; I've crept back into my life as if I had never left it. With each step, I remember, *this is where I live, this is my life*, here is where I fit.

The ocean bath at the south end of the beach is dirty, unswimmable, so I walk along the beach towards the north end. I am alone as I slide into the water, a cleansing *mikvah* of homecoming.

'I'm back,' I whisper.

'Oh you've returned?' Lin smiles from behind the deli counter.

I am touched that she remembers I have been in South Africa. I tell her my mother passed away while I was there. She says she is sorry, I thank her and ask for $10 of sliced chilli chicken. I dash into Woolworths for a few staples while her husband Charles slices it fresh.

When I return, Lin hands me a bunch of pink roses. 'For your mother.'

In that second, I understand that the people who provide you twice a week with all your charcuterie needs can be some of your favourite people, and the kindest too.

As I walk home clutching my roses, I remind myself not to tell random people about my mother's death. It is too precious to blurt out. But I feel wrong, not-me-anymore, other-like, and I am certain people can tell. I am sure it shows that I have been stripped of the one person who loved me the most.

The beach is closed because of a mighty swell heralded by the thunderstorm that kept me stalled in the airport terminal yesterday. I walk in the rain up to Wylies Baths, and dive into the wild waves where I frolic for an hour, my body surging with freedom and joy, as the salt scorches me, and I am held.

At last, at last, at last.

Zed texts me from the mountains: the Australian government has just announced that anyone who has been in South Africa in the past two weeks has to have a Covid test and self-isolate for fourteen days, irrespective of the outcome of the test. He ends with, 'Sorry, my love.' Omicron is what they're calling this new strain of Covid.

I can't help the tears. I'm home but not quite free. I chide myself to get a grip; at least I am back safely. I have Archie. I got to spend time with my kids. I've had two swims.

Suddenly, countries all over the world are shutting their borders to South Africa. The unknowns whip around me. Once again, I am far away and out of harm's way, but will my dad, sisters, friends, and all the people I love be safe from this new strain?

I am overwhelmed by the sense that this will never end, that we will just have to keep spinning in these endless loops of one pandemic after another. It's the same torturous cycle we were in with my mother, living from blood test to blood test, swinging between hope and despair, never knowing what tomorrow will bring.

I get my negative Covid result at 1.40 am.

It makes no difference; I have no choice but to self-isolate for two weeks.

I remain indoors, like someone recuperating from a medical procedure or long illness. The sun streams through the window in my study. I hear the sea calling me. I don't remember ever having pined for a romantic partner this much.

When Zed returns, I fall into his hug, though the cost is that he will have to isolate with me. I have been a lone particle since my mother died. Hugs by sisters and friends have been balm. But Zed is the one I have longed for. I had forgotten his smell, the olfactory trace of his personality. Skin hunger is what it's called when we are deprived of the specific touch of the ones with whom we co-regulate. With him home, I sleep again, almost normally.

He is back with me, my person, the one whose hand I reach for when I wake at night. I have missed this small act of intimacy over the past few months. My father kept telling us how he rubbed my mother's back for hours the night before she died. He was within arm's reach when she left.

I think to myself, God also loves my mother.

When I wake, Zed is fast asleep. I look at him frantically, like I am memorising him. I study his stubble, the shape of his nose, his shaved head, the hair on his arms, his tanned limbs from all that marathon running. Those fingers with the ring I once made for him when I did silversmithing all those years ago.

He opens his eyes.

'Hey, you okay?'

I nod.

'Are you crying?'

'Why would I be crying?'

'You were looking at me in an eerie way.'

'It's called love, Zed.'

We stay up way past midnight for a week binge-watching *Succession* and eating too much chocolate. I feel hungover every day. Linear time seems meaningless. I upend my rhythms, stay awake until all hours, sleep in, because in isolation, there are no circadian rhythms. I pine for the beach at sunrise, counting the days until I am free again.

A few friends call but I cannot speak on the phone.

I reread Roland Barthe's *Mourning Diary* and now, it is different. His words land in me in a completely new place.

'I no longer desire what I used to desire. I must wait… for a new desire to form, a desire following her death.'

I curl up in my study and tend to my sorrow alone, where I don't have to censor my emotions. The isolation has come as a blessing while I am not myself.

Over the following days and weeks, I start speaking to the dead.

'Mom, should I add paprika to this chilli con carne?' 'Where have I put my glasses?' 'Mom, why aren't you coming to me in my dreams?'

It feels oddly comforting to speak to her in this way now that I can no longer FaceTime or WhatsApp her. I keep photos of her close by. I think about where she has gone and if she can hear me. Sometimes I cry, great, heaving sobs. They come upon me, like symptoms of an illness over which I have no control. My heartache is not continuous— it is a relief as much as a confusion. It comes and goes. It is impossible to measure from day to day, hour to hour whether it is diminishing, or gaining force.

Each time it arises, it has the same inflamed intensity. But then it evaporates for a bit, and I think, ah, I'm getting over it.

All that has gone completely and utterly is my fear that she will die and leave me.

CHAPTER 25

A beehive grew under our kitchen floorboards while I was away. Now I can feel the heat from the hive under the tiles near our back door. A steady stream of bees flies in and out from an aperture under the floor. I am quite enchanted by this—that the bees have picked, of all places, this spot to make their home—though, of course, it is a big problem for our building.

I am speechless when the strata manager sends me names of exterminators. I do my own research to find an apiarist so that they can be rehomed safely. I book a guy to come look and see what can be done, but the following day, I find a heap of dead bees at our back door and, oh god, I start to cry at the sight of all those lifeless little bodies.

I wonder if this is the beginning of madness.

While I wait for the bee guy to arrive, I think about the poem the Spanish poet Antonio Machado wrote after he lost his young wife Leonor, about how he dreamed of a beehive in his heart and making 'sweet honey from old failures.' I feel wildly protective of these creatures who have chosen to build their home under my kitchen. I wonder what it means, you know, metaphorically. In Celtic mythology, bees are holders of wisdom, and they believed that bees travel between worlds, bringing messages from the gods. I am porous to these associations, almost desperate with need to make sense of things so they tie me back to my mother.

All I can think is: don't kill the queen.

I receive a Whatsapp from Laura: 'Do you know mom's Netflix password?'

All the intel has gone with her. The world is mottled and muddled with her absence.

Some days later, Laura and Carolyn fret—they can't find the purple Le Creuset pot we gave mom for her 70th birthday which Laura was hoping to take.

It's just a thing. I can't get worked up about things.

If my mother could disappear, why not a pot?

Our closest friends have a 'Welcome Home Shabbat' for me. It is just the right kind of adoring madness to ground me home. A sign WELCOME HOME JO, WE LOVE YOU hangs over their doorway, and the table is decorated with criss-crossing streamers.

Into the arms of these darling people, I am enfolded, returned to my life.

And just as I am receiving the comfort of this, Martha, a neighbour, asks, 'Was it a good trip?'

I stare blankly for a moment.

'Well, my mother died… so….'

'Yes, sorry to hear that, but other than that, was it a good trip?'

Do we even hear ourselves anymore, I wonder?

In a boutique jewellery store on the North Shore, the assistant takes out the trays of rings, and I slip one on, then another. I want to get it right; to put the last birthday money my mother gave me towards this investment, this lovely thing I will wear each day on my body and remember her by. I ask the advice of a woman standing next to me and she weighs in, though why we ask strangers to help us make important decisions in which they are uninvested, I can't explain. But our proximity gives me the occasion to eavesdrop, and she is here, she explains, to buy a ring for her mother for Christmas.

I tell myself, I will get better at this. I will not always devolve into unexplained tears because I will never again buy my mother a gift. Someday, I will just be able to be happy for a stranger who is purchasing a present for her mother, without envy or sadness.

It is clear I am not ready to be let out in public.

Over a morning coffee at our favourite beach cafe, Zed says, 'You look spare.'

All my self-confidence to step outside and be in public has vanished. I don't understand anymore how to be in my own body. I feel as if I have been disassembled and reassembled, and parts have been put back in the wrong place.

Day after day, I wake up to the weight of life without my mother. Once the exhilaration of disbelief passes, what's left is an exhaustion for life. I contemplate the word 'acedia' from Roland Barthes—the feeling of listlessness, torpor, not being concerned with one's position in the world. It comes with undirected anxiety, an inability to concentrate and no desire to do anything. As if nothing has any meaning.

I feel as if I'm unplugged and no longer charging, like my battery has run to empty. I only have small puffs of energy for essentials. I did not know that a mother is a socket, an outlet, a power point, who pulses vitality into us. But of course, it makes sense. The umbilicus is not only a biological fact, it must also come with a soul component.

Believing she is gone—that is the problem. It seems to boil down to this. I can only make sense of her death as fake news. My mind rationally knows the information is accurate, and I execute all the tasks and habits that make up my days, but then the glitch of grief disrupts everything again, like a fault in the system, and stalls me. But then, I restart. That's how we're built. That's how we go on.

I read Rilke—who says we must 'ripen death inside us.' I think maybe what he's saying is we have to come to believe in someone's death, because it is so inconceivable when it happens.

I call my father every day. One day he tells me he wakes up thinking he shouldn't cough too loudly because he doesn't want to disturb my mother and then he realises the bed next to him is empty. On another, he says he has no appetite—'I had a MasterChef cooking for me.' Now, each day is a drag. He has no lust for life anymore, and I understand that. I have to rev my engines each day—the only incentive I have for getting out of bed is going down to the ocean.

I tell my dad to get in the pool and swim.

A few months later, I am at Specsavers where the young assistants are enthusiastic and helpful. They enact a certain kind of care and attention that only a mother would offer:

'The smaller ones... yes the darker frames... I prefer the purple...'

They stand back and assess, offering their advice and opinions. Even if it's all in the name of customer service, I feel taken care of.

The young woman asks with great earnestness, as if a great deal hangs on my answer, 'Which ones do you feel more confident in?'

I can't help it. I devolve into laughter that is very close to tears. It's such a darling of a question. How do I tell her, 'The ones that can help me navigate the world without my mother'?

CHAPTER 26

Over the coming weeks, kind people send me things to read about grief and loss. There is, apparently, a whole industry of pop-psychology about how the dead send signs and how to look for them—through feathers, electricity and other household objects. Someone forwards me details of a medium and a book about what happens to the souls of the dead. Perhaps I should be more interested. I thank her and tell her I'm 'not following that path for now.' I understand why people do, but it's not for me. I don't want or need to imagine my mother floating above me in a ghostly form. I would find that creepy and intrusive. She was not a hoverer. She was respectful of my privacy in life, as I'm certain she would be in death, so even if she was offered the upgrade to aerial views of the ones left behind, I don't imagine she would take it.

Jess says, 'That's not who Nana was—expansive and overarching. Maybe she's hiding in the salt cellar, or the dental floss—a spirit of the small and useful things in life.'

I am not seeking comfort. No-one can tell me where she went. All I want is to orient myself in this journey of grief. How much longer will it feel like falling? When will I be at rock bottom? *I just want to know where I am,* as my mother tried to teach me in those last few weeks.

In the water, I call out to her, I shout her name into the sky. *I miss you, mama, can you hear me?*

I watch for signs.

Meanwhile, Covid numbers rocket into the tens of thousands. So many people are sick and in isolation, though we are mercifully out of lockdown. Still, it feels as if we are all biding our time, sitting it out, waiting for it all to be over. Will it be? Ever? All the restrictions and regulations, changed social behaviours, meetings over Zoom, drive-throughs for quick Covid tests, have been normalised. We have grown around them to accommodate this new way of being in the world. Travellers returning from South Africa now must spend two weeks at Howard Springs quarantine facility in Darwin.

Zed had a very different relationship with his mother, and despite how much he wants to support me, he is bewildered by my emotional collapse. He sometimes walks in, sees my face and asks, 'What's wrong?'

'My mother died,' I say.

'Oh… yep…' he nods. It has been months.

I ask him for the raw footage of my mother singing 'Sounds of Silence' for my 50th birthday video which he compiled. She didn't sing often, but now and then, after a few drinks, or when she was on holiday, she and my dad would burst into song—and she could hold a tune. These were glorious tears in the fabric of her taut control, when her spirit flickered. In their early years, my folks were yogi hippies who played guitars and sang songs like Joan Baez's 'Donna, Donna,' about a calf on a wagon bound for a market who asks why he can't instead be a swallow, wild and free, as the winds laugh, indifferent to his fate.

The song has always left me with my dad's gloomy Sunday feeling.

As I watch the video of her singing, I see what Zed saw. She sang sad. How did I miss that?

I cry over her, and for all the things taken from her—a sibling, a happy childhood, an easy parenting life, Jess, when we moved to Cape Town, then to Australia. Mostly I weep that she never got to see my kids again.

I find the video on my phone I took of her lighting Shabbat candles—as it turns out, it was the last time we'd get to do that ritual with her. She had berated me, 'Don't film this, Jo, it's nonsense.' I also recorded our conversation when she was in hospital, confused, potassium-deficient, girlish in her innocence as the prickly defensiveness of her personality peeled away. I watch these over and over, thinking how she never wanted to burden us, and she never did. She slid away, and how she loved us, went with her. My sorrow is not just about missing her; it is also about missing the way her love made me feel.

I start to become aware of a shelf life to this condition, not just other's tolerance for it, but my own. When is it 'enough'? I'm not looking for a bypass, shortcut, hack or secret corridor. I don't want to skirt or shirk the responsibilities of this heartache, with its undertow of sinking. It is like a rip current I dare not imagine I am equal to. But I don't want to feed off this loss forever. If I just keep unravelling it, I am certain I will eventually get to the end of grief's rope. Maybe grief evaporates slowly, no matter whether you're doing a mindful excavation of it, or whether you're on vacation from it, far away like Maisie who left Horton the elephant to hatch her egg. I am Horton. Sitting on this egg of grief, waiting for it to hatch, waiting for new life to emerge.

In conversations, people tell me about narcissistic, mean, cruel or absent mothers. Jennette McCurdy's memoir comes out, called; *I'm Glad My Mom Died* about her abusive mother. I read a poem by Barbara

Kingsolver called 'My Mother's Last Forty Minutes' about nursing her mother while she was dying. The poem ends with the line: 'Here begins my life as no-one's bad daughter.'

Some people do everything they can to get away from their mothers. I spent my life trying to reach mine, even from a distance.

Each day, I give my father my full attention when he calls. I listen to his heartaches and worries, and I console him. I tell him it will be okay. I have to mother him now. He is adamant he will not move from the house. He is comfortable in the familiarity of the space, living off the dregs of happiness, because rumours of our mother abide in the house; her kitchen is as she left it (maybe a little tidier); her garden is flourishing with all the rain, and the succulents I planted have exploded.

For the first time, he is alone on what would have been their sixtieth anniversary. When we speak, he is limp with exhaustion, as if life is just too many hurdles. 'I've run my race,' he sighs. 'And your mother's absence weighs heavily on me now.'

I tell him I am proud of how he has handled losing mom.

'It's harder to lose a mother than a partner,' he says.

The time is coming when he will have to move out of 60 The Braids Road, and it is a terrifying prospect. My sisters and I fret in the Sisters WhatsApp group, but what is to be done? We can't force him to do something he isn't ready for.

I notice I have become softer with him; my patience for him has grown.

He tells me he says a little prayer each day, 'Dear God, please exist.'

I only begin to feel it all, months later. The endings within endings that her ending entails. Grief is how I must love her now, and I start to trust that this shedding will slough away more than just my mother.

I begin to slowly peel my mother away from my daily life. It's a painstaking process of pulling off filaments of our lifelong interaction, by email, phone, WhatsApp.

My sisters begin to fill up the space in my heart that my mother occupied. Sometimes I wonder who of the three of us will die first, then second and who will be left—the last standing sister. I don't want to lose either of them, but I don't want them to have to lose me.

I call friends who lost mothers years ago and apologise for my insensitivity to their loss.

'I never knew…' I sob, 'I'm sorry, I never understood till now.'

Months on, I don't 'feel' my mother anywhere, except as a memory.

I wander around like that little bird in the P.D. Eastman children's book, asking every tree and fish and shaft of moonlight, 'Are you my mother?'

Nothing is.

CHAPTER 27

It is not something I share with my father, why would I? He's an old man, a widower, an orphan.

It was a freak accident. It is the first time in sixty years, I tell myself. The man was swimming alone, around a spot where fishermen were casting from the cliffs, which often attracts sharks. Still, a fatal attack by a great white off the Sydney coast shakes me cold. The beaches are closed while they search for the creature, though God knows what they will do with it if they find it.

My neighbour, an unbearable human being, announces loudly in his driveway that he has a photograph of the corpse, without limbs, 'he bled out fast.' He asks if I want to see it.

I shake my head. 'Definitely not. Don't show that around.'

That was a person—a diving instructor—with a fiancé and parents. His name was Simon Nellist.

The kids are all with us for dinner when we get the call that Zed's father, Jack, who was almost 97, has died. It's one of the only times I've seen Zed cry. How good and right it is that we are all together, because this is how it is meant to be. When we grieve, we are supposed to be with the people we love the most. We sit together and tell stories about Jack.

Zed leaves to fly back to South Africa to bury his dad.

While he's there, he joins my father and sisters at 60 The Braids Road for a meal of fish and chips. He messages me, 'Your mother's absence is enormous.' When we speak, he says it was almost unbearably difficult to be at the table without her. He misses how she used to sit there, a quiet, strong presence, overseeing the scrum for the food, and bringing a quiet grace to it all and telling people, 'It's enough' and 'shut up already,' when it was enough and time to shut up.

I realise it has only hit Zed now that my mother is really gone. His grief makes me feel a little less lonely in mine.

He returns from South Africa, bringing the dreaded virus with him. He is sick first and passes it on to me.

Covid takes over my whole body. It starts with a headache, a sore throat, and then, I am flattened. I cough and feel achy. I completely lose my sense of smell and taste. Coffee tastes like hot water. People are now reported to be suffering from Lo-Co, long Covid, a range of bizarre symptoms that never go away. If I have lost my smell and palate permanently, I don't know what I will make of a tasteless, odourless life. *Kill me now*, my mother would have said.

When I have the quiet apartment to myself, I type the names Sonali Derinyagala and Matt Golinski into Google—both of whom lost their whole families, Sonali in the tsunami in Sri Lanka and Matt in a house fire. It's inconceivable what they have had to endure—and a photo of Sonali's face shows that sorrow, as Matt's burns expose his agony. I don't know if that is triumph, but it is perseverance. And grace. I am awed at how they have both gone on to build new lives.

As Covid has its way with me, it squirms through a keyhole into my spirit. While the physical symptoms morph and decline, I am hollowed with certainty that my entire life has been a failure. I cannot shake it, no matter what affirmations I recite, prayers I offer up or meditations I close my eyes into. My mother would often tell me that 'it's common to feel depressed after you've been sick.' If she were here, she'd encourage me to go outside, get some Vitamin D, exercise, have a swim, a whiskey, a massage.

A dark existential anguish envelops me. I am drowning.

I wonder if I should cut all my hair off.

'What for? I love your long hair,' I imagine her saying.

Death mythologises people and I don't want to romanticise my mother, just to see her clearly, to know who she really was. I want to know what I got from her and who I learned to be, because often, while I was growing up, I thought I did not want to be anything like her. I trawl through old photographs, forensically examining all the bits and pieces my mother left behind, trying to understand who she was, not only as my mother, but as a person.

I have learned that people we love are bigger than any descriptions we can attach to them. They are more vibrant and mysterious than simply the roles they performed in our lives. After someone dies, you begin to see them in ways you couldn't when they were alive.

My favourite story about her is one I've been told, and so I have to imagine it. I've always believed my mother never lost her temper. But apparently, once, she did.

When Carolyn was little, my parents were at friends for the afternoon. My sister was playing on their son's bicycle. The son told her to get off his bike, which, of course, Carolyn didn't hear. The kid grabbed the handlebars and threw her off. When she fell and cut her knee, crying, the parents berated the boy in mild admonishment, 'Oh

Gavin, that wasn't a very nice thing to do.' And what did my shy mother do? She marched over to Gavin and she smacked him on his bottom.

You did not want to mess with her.

The day after the fatal shark attack, I stand on the shoreline looking out across the bay, with my goggles and cap. I do not go out as far out as I usually do, but I swim across that bay. This is both how I know I am not my mother and also that her fierceness lives inside me.

CHAPTER 28

I stare into the dark hours, wondering to whom I can tell my sorrow. I am pushed up to the very ends of myself. I've never known or understood depression until now. Life does not make sense anymore. Nothing inside me feels as if it will survive.

I confess to Zed that I am not doing well, that I am desperate, hopeless. I thought I was through the worst of it, but now, seven months after my mother's death, a stronger strain of grief assails me.

'Don't panic,' he consoles.

He takes me out in the dark to the rockpool beneath the Surf Lifesaving Club where I swim under the moon, in the bright night, tossed by waves that don't taste like anything, because Covid still holds my senses of smell and taste hostage. I dunk my head under the water and stay there until I have to come up for air. I want the water up my nose, to clear my nasal passages, maybe that will help me wean myself off the nasal spray I've been using which has caused a vicious rebound congestion. The more you use it, the less effective it is, and the worse it makes your congestion. So this is what I have—rebound grief.

'Why am I not getting better?' I ask Zed.

'Just swim,' he encourages.

It is a cloudy Easter Saturday, and I am stretched out on the beach after a few laps across Coogee Bay, Zed by my side. It is a day to pay special attention to the flags. Just by looking at the ocean, you wouldn't suspect the force of the rip at the north end, which can carry you far out in a flash as the waves that crash to shore find their way back. I warned Zed when he went in for a dip, having just swum out of it myself.

Sitting on the sand, I am vaguely conscious of an elderly man entering the shallows. No more than a minute or two passes, when I see a raised arm far out in the water, and his wife begins to shout for help. The lifeguards are up the south end of the beach, and there is no time. I spring to my feet and dash into the surf and swim as hard and fast as I can towards him, the surge of the rip backstroking me further and further out. As I do, a swimmer approaches from the south. I call out to the man in trouble, 'Are you okay?' and 'Don't panic.'

Between us, the other swimmer and I instruct him to swim across. We guide him towards us, encouraging him, *you're doing well* and *stay calm, you're going to be okay*. We coach him out of the rip, tell him not to pull on us, and then we reach out our arms to let him hold onto us as we swim him towards the shore together.

As we stagger onto the beach, a lifeguard comes running towards us. But it's too late. We've done the job, though not as skilfully as I might have done—in my haste, I'd forgotten to grab the lifebuoy dangling from the post precisely for such eventualities.

Zed looks at me incredulously.

'That was impressive. I don't know how you did that.'

The immensity of what I have just done falls upon me, as the man and his wife shower me with thanks and praise. 'It was nothing,' I say. But it is, in fact, huge. I didn't save his life—the lifeguards would have gotten to him if I hadn't. But maybe I just saved my own. In that moment, I had strength and clarity of purpose. I knew

I could navigate that rip and help someone in distress. It feels like a sign, an antidote to the despair of the past few weeks. My life is worth something.

I wonder, in the big picture of my destiny, if all this swimming, just like my years of spiritual work, have been training, just so I could do this one thing.

In preparation for Passover, I turn to my mother's *kneidlach* recipe in her 80th birthday celebration book.

'Eggs, matza meal, oil, salt, pepper, shmaltz,' it reads.

Not a single measurement. I laugh out loud. She cooked by instinct—just as I do. I cannot tell you how much oil, mustard or honey I put in my salad dressing—I just keep tasting and adding ingredients until it's right.

I am left to decipher her free-range recipes and try to listen to the absences she left behind. Two or three eggs? A quarter cup of oil or half a cup? In that quiet unknowing, I have to raise her from the dead and feel all the ways in which she lingers—an intuition, a sensibility, an inclination towards the delicious and the slightly too-salty.

Weeks before she died, she stood beside me at the stove, bent over from nausea from the chemotherapy, as her ruby grapefruit marmalade bubbled on the stove, and when I asked her how long it needed to boil, she held out a spoon and said, 'When it gets to *this* consistency, you know it's ready.'

The Germans have a beautiful word *Eigenzeit*, which means 'the time inherent to a process itself.' As it is with marmalade, so it is with grief.

Don't time it. Don't leave it to burn. Keep an eye on it. You'll know when it's done.

This first year without her is hardly the time by which to judge the loss. Joan Didion described it as the year of magical thinking. The untortured silent truth of her absence in perpetuity is dropping in. Mostly, I accept it as real; I am starting to believe it. But now and then, a small cry from within erupts: *Did you really die, mom? Did you really?*

My fear of being separated from her has come to its final rest at last.

But I also see that it is possible to lose a person you have loved from the beginning of time, without regret and devastation.

I have been writing letters to my mother for almost two years. I began the day she was diagnosed with cancer. Now, when I skip a day, I feel guilty—as if I am losing my connection to her. When my fingers are moving across the keys, I can imagine that she is on the receiving end of my words, that somehow, we are communicating like we did when she was alive over email, then WhatsApp messages.

I start to mourn grief's ending and what that will finish between me and my mother. Who will I be when this deep sadness shallows? Will I remember her less? I wonder what it is to 'just let it go,' as my father consoled the day after she died, in that gesture of his palm opening. I hope it has nothing to do with forgetting.

As I taste the food and try to work out if it needs more salt, I think of the author May Sarton's words, 'But now her truth is given me to live.'

Maybe there is something about the nine-month mark that is significant. The seal on the vacuum of my grief slackens slightly. The edges start to lift and trickles of light and oxygen return.

And I finally start to dream of her.

PART 5
GOING ON

CHAPTER 29

I make the error of checking my phone at 4 am, a habit I have not overcome since my mother's illness.

An earthquake has torn through Turkiye and Syria.

The death toll is at 23,000.

Images of the rubble and the dead and dying are all over social media. It feels like it cannot be true, despite the evidence in front of my eyes.

I turn off the light and feel Archie huddle into my side. I have no hopes of getting any more sleep.

But then, it sneaks in and pulls me far out into a dream where I wake up in the bedroom of my childhood home at 60 The Braids Road. I am a visitor, on a holiday like I was for so many years. I wander into my mother's bedroom. And there she is, sitting at her dressing table with her back to me. Oh my God, she is here, it is her. I am overcome with joy, that no, she hasn't died, she is still with us. I sit down on my father's bed and reach out for her.

'Mom, why did you have to leave us?' I ask, sobbing. I finally have her in front of me, I am talking to her, touching her.

And she turns to look at me, a small vexation on her face.

'Oh Joanne, do you think I wanted to?' she asks with an exasperated expression I know so well.

I am conscious that I am dreaming, and I wait because she's about to say something, and I know it is a profound message from another realm I will carry with me forever.

At last, she speaks, only four words which make complete sense in the way things do in a dream as history and foreknowledge of a future beyond grief find their way to one another like twin souls, and my glorious, green-eyed mother tells me:

'Save yourself for lunch.'

A year after her death, I am back at 60 The Braids Road. I have brought Jess and Aidan to South Africa for what may very likely be their final visit. Covid is not quite behind us, but many of the strict protocols are relaxed, now that we know 'where we are.' Most of us have had vaccines and contracted the virus itself. It still hovers among us, a spooky presence, reminding us that we can take nothing for granted.

The kids are quiet, estranged from this country in which they were both born, and from all the relationships from which we exiled them. I am trying hard not to project my sadness onto them, but I am certainly failing.

We drive on a Sunday morning to the cemetery to visit my mother's gravesite. We clear the weeds, wash the tombstone and plant new succulents. I want my children's hands to be reddened with the soil, so they know what it means to be stained by the loss of someone you love.

Later, we are gathered at my mother's dining room table for lunch. My father asks to see my tattoo—Carolyn's birthday gift to me which I had inked just yesterday.

I come stand beside him at his place at the head of the table and show him my left forearm. I know he doesn't approve of tattoos; it has to do with the numbers Nazi's tattooed on Jews in the Holocaust. But this is something I have chosen—the only mark on my body worthy of a lifetime of having to wear it.

My father nods.

'It's special.'

I squeeze his shoulder.

I had scoured my mother's diaries to find the four words in her handwriting. The tattoo artist put them together.

'*I love my life.*'

In the kitchen, I am looking for ingredients for a salad dressing to go with our lunch.

My mother's clutter has been cleared, the mess of her has been turned into a motherless order of bare necessities to keep my father in three-meals-a-day. I pretend like this is just perfectly okay.

I rifle through the cupboard. Surely not? I take everything out. How's it possible? Where is the olive oil? I open the pantry she always kept filled to the brim, and all I find are a few tins of tuna, baked beans and bags of coffee. In a year, Nomusa and my father have worked through all her stockpiled items we used to joke would see us through Armageddon. I check the fridge, for no sensible reason but confirmation of where I am and what is happening around me. I knew I'd never again find marinated fried eggplants, anchovies wrapped around olives, things stuffed with blue cheese, egg mayonnaise, chopped herring or that raw fish in lemon with slivers of onion and bay leaves. Those were her marks, her food-prints I always imagined would leave a trace, like the indentation on a pillow a cat leaves after a nap.

But the realisation is a thunderclap that splices me, that this is no longer my mother's kitchen.

I buckle against the kitchen counter, my breath a-shudder. I let myself cry in front of this stripped cupboard, this denuded fridge, great silent gulps that someone can be so gone. Even the one remnant of them you were certain you would find left behind, the ghostly indentation of their existence has been erased, not by violence but in the benign way in which things move on. In the ruins of my mother's kitchen, everything familiar has become strange, and I realise, shockingly, that the strangeness of her death is becoming familiar, a place I know well.

I rest there, bent over and wait for the wave of anguish to move through me. And when it does, I wash my face in the sink before I join the family around the dining room table for lunch, reminding myself to buy the best olive oil for Nomusa and my father before I leave.

CHAPTER 30

I need a good reason to enter the Twilight Zone that is Officeworks.

A new mouse for my computer is why I'm here, but my real mission is to print off a photograph of my mother. In it, she is resting her chin on her right palm, and she looks relaxed as she always did at the end of a meal. I want a large print to frame for my study.

I wait in a long queue as staff behind the counter avoid eye contact with customers while attending to printing orders. I get hopeful as I see someone in uniform approach the counter, but he meanders off, perhaps on a lunch or semi-urgent bathroom break, unapologetic, unhurried, as if time means nothing and all of us shmucks idling in single file between the staplers and highlighters on special, have more than enough of it. Eventually, a young man—Simon according to his large name tag, ushers me to the photo machines and talks me through how I can order a picture by following the prompts. It has been entirely unnecessary to stand in line for half an hour, he smiles, ruefully.

'Oh well, next time I'll know...'

Simon pulls up the photograph. My mother looks luminous, her green eyes are smiling, her lips are slick pink with post-dinner lipstick. You can see it in her smile; she is with her grandchildren in Australia.

'That's a beautiful picture,' he says.

His words catch me by surprise. For a moment, I cannot speak as tears constrict my throat.

'That's my mum. She passed away last year.'

I don't know what Officeworks pays their staff per hour. Or whether an emotional intelligence test forms part of the job application in the event of the grief-stricken needing to print photos of recently lost loved ones, but somehow, by divine grace, this dear man lands beside me in an overly bright warehouse of stationery and office goods. What he asks next is way beyond his paygrade or role.

'Did she have a good life?'

In an entire year since I have lost her, no-one has ever asked this pure and honouring question. I pause. How does one measure a life? By accomplishments? Wealth? Fame? Length? On none of these scales would my mother have scored, except maybe length. And even though she wasn't ready to die, she didn't die young. She had been lonely as a child, but she did not die a lonely death; she was surrounded by people who loved her. She had never been hungry or poor. She'd never sent a husband or a child to war. She'd borne some unbearable heartbreaks, but she'd never lost a child, nor a spouse. She'd been well most of her life. When cancer got her, it got her quickly. She died nine months after her diagnosis, in her bed next to her husband, in her sleep.

'Yes, thank you, I think she did,' I reply as hot tears fall down my cheeks.

As I stand in front of the printing machine with Simon, I look down at my healed tattoo, in my mother's unmistakable script, her capital 'I's with an upper loop, a flourish I have started to copy in my own handwriting. People who notice, often comment on it, *what a beautiful affirmation* and each time, I get to tell the story—that these are not my words, but my mother's, in the final weeks of her life when she took stock and summed it all up. Now I carry her precis, an incantation, a blessing that breaks the spell of all curses, all despairs tangled up in my grandmother's 'it's no good.'

'That's lucky,' Simon says. 'I'm so close to my mum, and I can't imagine losing her. I'm so sorry, it must be very hard.'

I watch him as he presses all the correct prompts on the screen to make sure I get the right size image.

There is a fantasy I have in which a daughter arrives at her mother's home after a long time away, like that Zen story of the young woman Chi'en, who runs away to marry the man she loves and returns many years later to make peace with her ageing father.

In my dream, the grandmother, who is old, opens the door, and the children who have become adults in a faraway land are awkward, and she is shy even in the hugs they share at that threshold before she invites them in. They do not remember how she held them when they were small and read them Dr Seuss and watched *Teletubbies* with them; but she remembers every fine detail.

The years have wrought changes in each of them, but she says, 'welcome,' and 'what can I get you?' They are polite and don't want to be any trouble; they'll have 'whatever is easiest.' She leads them into her kitchen and shows them they can have whatever they wish, for she has filled the table and the cupboards and the fridges with all manner of refreshments. They have travelled a long way to celebrate with her, and how lucky is she to have them with her? How lucky is she?

Around this table, I have gathered all the frayed threads of my family and woven them together. Here I dream my mother's lost eightieth birthday celebration. As they fill their plates with all the delicacies she made for them as children, and they taste her food, the distance shortens, and they begin to remember a time before, and the space the years have put between them shrinks. And she calls them, 'Lovey,' and they say, 'Nana, may I have some more?' and that question is a doorway to her heart and her smile, and she says, 'Of course.'

And what you have here are people known to one another, by blood, not time and though I have robbed her of all the years of being a grandmother if we had stayed, the room is filled with stories, both new and ancient, but without doubt, everyone feels it, the nearness of love and its spontaneous renewal that happens between people who are forever braided in the thick weave of kinship that outlasts all separations. The inverse of *Distance from. Can't get to. Out of reach.*

Right here.

Within reach.

Returned to.

Over the winter of 2022, I read Rebecca Gigg's book *Fathoms* about the lives and death of whales and their cultural, mythic and spiritual place in our world. The book has been next to my bed for ages. I dip in and out of it when I can concentrate at night instead of dulling myself with Netflix. I savour her meticulous research and beautiful writing in small increments.

I learn about whale song, the impact of climate change, sonic blasting, plastic pollution on cetacean wellbeing and *whalefall*—that word alone, a delight. And this is what I discover: when a whale dies, its carcass begins the long, slow descent to the ocean floor over a long period of time. As it does so, its body feeds tens of thousands, maybe millions of other creatures, giving back, giving back. Not a skerrick of whale goes to waste. Every microscopic bit of it, from its blubber to its flesh to its bones, is reabsorbed by other creatures. The death of a whale is a blessing to the entire ecosystem of the ocean, and in turn, to the whole planet.

If it is true of a whale's death, might the same be true of each of our dying? Can we, in our death, break into a million blessings?

In 2018, a female orca whale called Tahlequah, gave birth to a calf in the northeastern Pacific Ocean after an eighteen-month pregnancy, the first birth in her pod for three years. But the baby died soon after its birth. Instead of letting it sink, the mother orca nudged her calf's body through the water, for seventeen days, balancing it on her head and the tip of her nose. For all this time, she pushed the weight of her baby for dozens of miles each day, picking up the body as it sank, and hoisting it out the water, over and over again.

Biologists concluded that what we were witnessing was the mother grieving—she was not ready to say goodbye to her baby.

After two and a half weeks, exhausted from the effort, Talequah finally let go.

Two years later, she gave birth to a healthy baby calf.

My mother wasn't one for grandiose philosophies. She was a simple, grounded, down-to-earth person. She seldom gave life advice. But three months after we'd immigrated, she sent me an email after I'd written to tell her I'd spent the day looking at old photographs and crying. The subject of the email is 'don't cry.'

'Jo my baby, please don't cry. When you're feeling low the worst thing you can do is look at pictures or listen to African music. That is like sticking a knife through your heart. I know because I felt like that when you left for Cape Town. The best way to cope is to do other things constantly and keep your mind busy. Try to go to gym every day (a good stress reliever) and do yoga and Pilates if possible. …

Did I ever tell you how it was at the time Carolyn was diagnosed as hard of hearing? Things were so bleak and I was so sad and thought I would never smile again. That's how it felt—literally NEVER smile again. But nothing lasts forever, the bad things as well as the good. I think the time will come when you are happy again, mark my words. When Pa died I thought I would never get over it. It took about four years but suddenly I realised one day that I was not as heartbroken as I had been and it did gradually get better… Meantime, (be strong and don't look at photos). Love Mom.'

I know the time is coming for me to mark her words, and to love each tender moment of my life that offers itself; the light on the cat's whiskers; the toasted curry leaf undertones in each mouthful of dhal; the feeling of the breeze through the window.

I begin to feel the exhaustion of sorrow leaving me, and the longing to stop pushing my grief through the water, like Talequah did.

CHAPTER 31

It's the first summer after Covid regulations have been suspended, and we are free to roam without obligatory masks, hand sanitising and social distancing. Life begins to resemble what we call 'normal', and everyone I know is manically planning overseas trips and venturing out like we all just got a reprieve on a death sentence. I can't work out if we've changed for the better, or if this rebound consumption, fortified like a relapsed addiction, is proof that we're incapable as a species of doing anything differently.

In this season of 'carpe diem' and frantic adventure, I find myself in a new kind of lockdown, far from the arousals of our restored freedoms. It's not a physical affliction, but it's as though all my senses are all blunted. Nothing feels fully alive. In this state, it is bright as an exit sign inside me. I have arrived at the close of something.

I tell Zed, 'I'm finished with writing.'

The path of writing I stepped onto when I was six years old, penning stories and notes to my mother, which I followed into my teens with journal entries and then made into my vocation through books over the past three decades, has come to a dead end. The one practice I have always loved and leaned on to wrestle meaning no longer works. The bold brushstrokes of that impulse, much like a midlife libido, have thinned to a barely visible pencil drawing. I have nothing left to say. That's all there is to it. You can call it writer's block if you like. I've even stopped writing letters to my mother—after five hundred pages, I was done. Like she did, words have left me.

One death, it seems, hides others.

'We'll see,' Zed says. 'Give it time.'

I am sitting out the summer by staying cloistered all day in the apartment after I return from sunrise swims. From the window in my study, I can hear the heaving, sweltering cacophony of holiday makers in their sarongs and budgie smugglers, carting their Acai's, iced lattes and vapes down to the beach, traces of which will be left as leisure litter for the council to deal with later.

I only love my suburb when the crowds leave—mostly during the autumn and winter months, when the sun is a quiet merciful nurturance, the beach sparsely populated and from under their puffy jackets and beanies, people call you 'mad' for swimming. It's a secret I hope the masses never catch onto—that there is nothing as divine as winter swimming, in water warmer than the ambient temperature, rounded off with the climax of endorphins as the body toggles between shiver and thaw.

Right now, everything is too much. The water is too warm, the air too hot, and even the fan cannot alleviate the stifle. In the seclusion of my study, I play Nick Cave's *Ghosteen* on repeat, an album he wrote after his son Arthur died tragically in 2015, a kind of background soundtrack to get me through the fuckfest that is the festive season. Zed doesn't like the songs. He finds them weird and haunting; it's exactly why I'm drawn to them.

Piled up on the daybed are books by the children's author, Kate di Camillo. I am joined by Archie, and though I am being roasted by his snuggling, I can't bring myself to push him away. Besides, I need the oxytocin.

Each book takes me an hour to read, the print is large, and there are pictures. This is as much exertion as I can garner as I slip into these children's stories about courageous mice and squirrels with superpowers and China rabbits. *The Magician's Elephant,* is about an orphan, Peter Augustus, who sets off on a journey to find his lost sister, upon the mysterious injunction of a fortune teller, 'You must follow the elephant,' a directive that makes no sense in a world in which there are no elephants. Yet.

Creative propagation doesn't happen often, but this little tale about impossible magic and strange encounters does something of a CPR to the part of me that is frozen. Like a heartbeat restored, or a narrative graft from a donor, circulation returns to my writing parts. And just like that, words begin to tick back into me.

Within days, I have written the first three chapters of a children's book, *The Whale's Last Song,* about a little girl without a mother, who goes in search of a cure for her pox-infected sister during a pandemic. It is written in a voice I do not recognise as my own and is filled with wondrous characters, including a wounded soldier, a blind old woman and a whale returning to the bay in which it was calved, to die.

Grief, it seems, is a mystery too vast to face head-on. Imaginary realms are easier to navigate than our own stark loss. Rabbi Nachman of Breslov believed it was only stories that could awaken us and help us keep our wounded hearts open when it seems no medicine will heal us. Fairytales and fiction allow us to borrow hope and sorrow from a fabled elsewhere, passing on secrets of the soul buried in their mythic arcs.

Only now do I understand what the author Sharon Blackie meant when she wrote that, 'grief is an element of enchantment.' The death of someone we love is an aching portal to a richly felt life, altering us into seeing the world in all its pain and wonder and deepening our connection to everything around us.

In the Buddhist story 'A Handful of Mustard Seeds', the subject of Nick Cave's song, 'Hollywood', on the album *Ghosteen,* Kisa Gotami's baby son dies. She goes to the Buddha, who promises to bring him back to life if she returns with a handful of mustard seeds from a house which has been untouched by grief. Door to door, she is met with the heartache of others and so, becomes enlightened when she understands that everyone, without exception, is touched by loss.

Stories help us grapple with questions that have no neat answers or solutions, like 'how can we bear this life full of loss and sorrow when we cannot save the people we love?' Stories offer us a track by which to find our way home, like the trail of breadcrumbs in Hansel and Gretel; or six letters written by a daughter; or the journey to find a magician's elephant and a missing sister.

I could not save my mother. Not with a message in a bottle, daily prayers, energetic healing, Turkey Tail mushrooms, chicken soup or a garden filled with flowers that propagate.

Instead, I wrote about a little girl who tries to rescue her sister, and in doing so, learns about the mother she lost and the whale that saved her.

As I stand back now, some distance from it all, and cast my eyes over the maddening, heart-shattering days we lived through, not only as a species, but as a little family losing our anchor, I sometimes wonder, like Louisa Durrell, *What was it all for?*

And I think of Spiro's answer: *'Would you have missed it if you'd known?'*

CHAPTER 32

My kids have invited me over for Mother's Day lunch. They're cooking. It's a surprise and no, I can't bring anything, just an appetite.

It's autumn here now. The summer crowds have thinned, and the water has a delicious icy bite. The clouds crouch low in the sky, making it overcast. Rain is forecast for later. I like it. The beach only draws the die-hards now.

After a few days of heart-thumping swell, the waves so huge they engulfed Wedding Cake Island, the bay is calm and clear again. You just never know what you're going to find when you get down here. Every day is a wild surprise.

The yearning for my mother has lost its burn. I miss her now with the same quality of separation as when she lived halfway across the world from me. Her absence has become part of my waters. I live with the ache as a kind of perpetual dull sorrow in my marrow. I sometimes try to feel for it, to be close to her again, just to experience the shock once more. I once touched an electric fence on purpose just to see what it would feel like. It is a lot worse than you expect, which I suppose is the point.

My life here in Coogee, so close to the ocean, has changed who I am. It has formed me, the way parents shape a child with their personalities, moods, presence and absence. I am this swimming self only because of this place, this water, this land. There is a name for this, I've discovered: topophilia, the tenderness we feel for a special place. I have started to listen, and where I am is showing me how to belong to it.

I swim out with strong strokes, hugging the rocky ridge on the south of Coogee Bay towards McIvers Ladies Baths. The cold runs over my shoulders, down the nape of my neck, the spot that converts a dip into a proper swim. Your whole-body flinches at the anticipation of it but settles as soon as the water meets it. I dive down to stroke the sway of the seagrass beneath me, like running fingers through a beloved child's hair. Then I head across the bay, north, catching the water with slightly parted fingers, my pulse heavy in my throat, as I snatch short breaths over each shoulder. It's a short 350 metres, not a kilometre as I first imagined before I ever attempted to swim the bay, and with the Bali memorial in sight ahead of me, I stop and turn to look back at the beach about a hundred metres in front of me.

I spin onto my back to catch my breath. I pull my goggles off to see everything clearly. This is the bay around which I have made my life here in Australia. These are the waters in which my children have learned to swim between the flags and dive through waves. This is the geography of my exile, the place that rehomed me and gave me a new life.

My life has become a story of water; I no longer think of myself as separate from it. I have sunk into the ocean's dreaming. When I am far from the sea, I am homesick for it. I have never belonged to any place more than I do in these waters. Over the past year, my lifeforce has flowed back into me like a new tide.

'Where are you, mama?' I call out to the attending sky.

The water laps around me as I tread it. It stretches deep and mysterious beneath me, and I am so small I could easily vanish.

I turn to look back at the beach. The ocean belongs to no-one, and yet, everyone and everything is beholden to its wild secrets.

Phytoplankton pumps oxygen into the atmosphere, the waters abound with life-giving nutrients, imagine food without salt (my mother couldn't); envisage life without immersion (I couldn't). It is made of and for living things. A cuttlefish can heal your heart. A Port Jackson shark, your hollowing sorrow. No-one quite understands how whale songs in one place are replicated across the globe. And why would we want to? There is so much we do not know and never will.

In this moment, I am being rocked by the muscle of the ocean's body against mine, and I feel part of whatever all this means. It is here that I touch a long ancestral heritage, deeper than blood family, broader than human bodies, an alchemy of rock and wind and water and fish and crustacean and mammal. Heaven, I believe, will be something like this sloshing, dreamy, salt-winded, light-speckled, enfolding vastness.

'I love and miss you,' I call out. 'I'll miss you forever, you know that?'

I think now of her, sinking like a whale carcass through all the layers of consciousness, memory, nostalgia and dreaming, spawning new life the deeper she drops. Could her death have been a godsend? Has her dying made space for new blessings to hatch? As she begins to fall apart and splinter, I feel as if I am losing her, the 'her' I knew as 'my mother.'

But it is, I have discovered, impossible to grieve while you are swimming.

I wait for a sign. Perhaps the clouds will part, and the sun will stream through. A seagull? A cormorant? Something that will let me imagine, 'Ah, yes, there she is.'

Nothing. Not even the wind picks up.

I pull my goggles back over my eyes and start to swim back towards the beach, letting the current carry me, mindful that the weather is brewing something wild for later.

I am passing over the rocks at the north end of the bay, when I see something pink flash beneath me. I have seen flares of neon purple seaweed, vermillion coloured seagrass, orange, white and black striped clownfish, iridescent flashes on a rainbow fish as the sun catches it before. Never pink.

I dive down and close my hand over the object.

As I surface, I remove my goggles to see what I am holding.

It's a heart-shaped rock, dyed bright fuchsia pink. One of those gimmicky stones you find in shops that sell dreamcatchers and incense.

This seems too literal and I start to laugh.

'I wish I believed in all that stuff,' she always claimed.

It's okay. She didn't have to believe in God for me to take this as a sign, that tomorrow, and the next day, I must rise and face my sorrow again. I must make something beautiful of every day—a swim, a soup, a poem.

I will love my life because of her, and through every small thing she taught me.

I clasp the stone in my hand and swim back to shore, my strokes long and sure.

I still have to shower and get dressed to be in time for my celebration. I don't want to keep my kids waiting.

I'm saving myself for lunch.

AFTERWORD

On 23 December 2024, I rushed from Sydney to be at my father's bedside as he began to slip away. An infection got hold of him, and the antibiotics just couldn't do their job any longer. Over ten days, I sat vigil at his bedside with my sisters and his angelic carers, playing his favourite Leonard Cohen songs, whispering last words of love and comfort into the giant elephant flaps of his ears and rubbing his size 12 feet. Three months earlier, he had sold 60 The Braids Road and moved into an aged care facility. When he got there, he told Nomusa not to unpack his books. He didn't think he'd last very long. He knew when it was 'no good.'

On his deathbed, the palliative care doctor asked him:

'How are you feeling?'

'I've been worse,' he joked.

I promised I would find a home for his massive body of work in a public source archive so it can continue to be enjoyed as part of the commons.

'So many promises,' he said. 'I just want a Coke.'

After my mother died, he told me, ''I wish I could find the off switch.'

On 11 January 2025, ten days shy of his 85th birthday, he finally did.

On 14 December 2025, when I was working on the edits of this manuscript, two gunmen opened fire on a Chanukah celebration at Bondi beach, killing fifteen people, most of whom were Jews. The safety of Australia, which I had always taken for granted, was shattered. Amidst my shock, anger and grief, I was grateful neither of my parents were alive to witness this turn of events. I am glad my mother died believing we lived in Paradise and that the sacrifices of immigration had brought her grandchildren to a land of safety.

In its wake, I have felt the dissolution of an incarnation shift, to a new instar, this time, to an awakening that we are always swimming against the rip of sorrow. Perhaps it is ultimately, the only truth to which we belong.

ACKNOWLEDGEMENTS

I have been held by the love and care of Zed, my children Jess and Aidan, my sisters Carolyn and Laura, niece Jenna, Carolyn's stepdaughter Jayne, beloved carers Nomusa and Bridget, cousins Charlene and Sandra, brothers-in-law David and Jeremy, and dear friends Lewis, Angela, Theo, Tracey, Graeme, Lesley, Audrey, Ilze, Kaaren, Wiremu, Lorraine, Tanya, Tracy C, Janine and Suzie through the loss of my mother. Lewis walked me through the sacred corridors of this loss, offering his emotional and architectural skills and support with boundless generosity. Suzie Miller understood this journey intimately, and held my hand, shared information and walked me through dark moments, with insight and humour.

Thank you to the brilliant and visionary Debbie Lee at Ginninderra Press, who jumped at the chance to publish this book and for being such a champion of this little grief story.

I was lucky to have the talented author and editor Katia Arial's editorial eye and heart on my words. Her insights and suggestions helped me edit 82,000 words down to 60,000 and to stay unswerving in a circuitous landscape. My mother would have approved. Thank you too, to Ruth Rosen for her careful eye over the manuscript and for tightening the little screws in invisible places, and Graham Davidson for this exquisite layout

I am grateful to my agents Jeanne Ryckmans and Anjanette Fennel from Key People Literary Management and Darryl

Samaraweera from Arteles Literary Agency in the UK, who have supported me during these difficult years.

Daniel Giovanno understood the brief for the cover and produced this beauty, which includes the Coogee shoreline on the back, a map of the waters in which I swim daily.

To the cats, Archie and Smudge, and all the creatures of the ocean who soothed me with their presence, I give my deep thanks for reminding me of my place in the greater family of all beings.

FURTHER READING

Bailey, Elisabeth Tova, *The Sound of a Wild Snail Eating*, Text Publishing, (2011)

Barthes, Roland, *Mourning Diary,* Hill & Wang, (2012)

Bernhard, Toni, *How to Be Sick: A Buddhist Inspired Guide for the Chronically Ill and their Caregivers,* Wisdom Publications, (2018)

Cave, Nick and O'Hagan, Sean, *Faith, Hope and Carnage*, Text Publishing, (2022)

Chalquist, Craig, *Terrapsychological Inquiry: restorying our relationship with nature, place and planet*, Routledge, (2024)

De Hennezel, Marie, *Intimate Death: how the dying teach us how to live,* Knopf, (1997)

Deraniyagala, Sonali, *Wave*, Vintage, (2013)

Di Camillo, Kate, *The Magician's Elephant,* Walker Books, (2015)

Egan, Kerry, *On Living*, Penguin Random House (2016)

Gershman, Nancy and Thompson, Barbara E, *Prescriptive Memories in Grief and Loss: The art of dreamscaping*, Routledge, (2019)

Hillesum, Etty, *An Interrupted Life: the diaries and letters of Etty Hillesum 1941—1943,* Persephone Books, (1999)

Hollis, James, *Hauntings,* Chiron Publications, (2013)

    Living with Borrowed Dust, Sounds True, (2025)

    On This Journey we Call our Life, Inner City Books, (2003)

    Swamplands of the Soul, Inner City Books, (1996)

Jenkinson, Stephen, *Die Wise,* North Atlantic Books, (2015)

Kubler-Ross, Elizabeth, *On Death and Dying*, Tavistock Publications, (1970)

Levine, Stephen, *A Year to Live*, Three Rivers Press, (1997)

Lewis, C S, *A Grief Observed*, Faber & Faber, (1961)

Moreland Johns, Fran, *Dying Unafraid*, Synergistic Press, (1999)

Partridge, Frances, *Other People Diaries 1963—1966*, Flamingo, (1994)

Prechtel, Martin, *The Smell of Rain on Dust,* North Atlantic Books, (2015)

Rabbi Nachman's Stories, Breslov Research Institute, (1983)

Rapp, Emily, *The Still Point of the Turning World*, Two Roads, (2013)

Rilke, Rainer Maria, *The Book of Hours,* Riverhead Books, (1996)

The Dark Interval: Letters for the Grieving Heart, Bloomsburg Publishing, (2018)

Tsui, Bonnie, *Why We Swim,* Penguin Random House, (2020)

Wardley, Tessa, *The Mindful Art of Wild Swimming*, Leaping Hare Press, (2017)

Weller, Francis, *The Wild Edge of Sorrow*, North Atlantic Books, (2015)

Wolynn, Mark, *It Didn't Start with You: how inherited family trauma shapes who we are and how to end the cycle,* Vermilion, (2022)

Nichols, Wallace J, *Blue Mind: how water makes you happier, more connected and better at what you do,* Abacus Books, (2015)

WATER SAFETY AND BASIC SWIMMING TIPS

Learning to swim is one of the greatest gifts we can give to ourselves. It is an empowering life skill and has many physical and mental health benefits.

Before we can swim in the ocean, we must first be **confident swimmers in a pool.**

This means we must be comfortable:

- putting our face in the water
- floating on our back
- swimming 50 metres unsupported by a flotation device (no matter the stroke).

The ocean is unpredictable due to waves, tides, currents, rips and wildlife. Safety should always be our priority when we swim.

STAYING SAFE AT THE BEACH

1. Always swim at a beach where there are lifeguards on duty. They are usually on patrol between 7 am – 7 pm. Swim between the red and yellow flags which is the area lifeguards have designated as the safest on that day.
2. Before entering, look for any signs on the beach to help you understand the conditions.
3. Take a bit of time to observe the water as well as the other swimmers. The conditions are different every single day and can change in a moment. Winds can come up, currents can change, sea creatures can appear suddenly.

4. Never swim alone. If you get into trouble in the water, it's important that there are people about to assist you.
5. Tell someone where you are going so they can keep an eye out for you.
6. Don't swim at dusk or at night.
7. Never swim intoxicated or under the influence of drugs or alcohol as they impair our assessment of danger.
8. Even on a cloudy day, make sure to protect yourself from the sun. Use an ocean-friendly sunscreen such as Feel Good Inc made free of toxic chemicals which harm ocean life.
9. Plan your entry and exit. Waves come in 'sets.' Enter the water in the lulls between sets.
10. The best way to handle a wave is to dive through or duck under it. You will feel a rush over your head as the wave passes.
11. When in doubt, get out. If for any reason you don't feel safe in the water, exit as soon as possible. If you are struggling to exit, put your hand up and the lifeguards will come and escort you out safely.
12. Always keep your wits about you and never turn your back on the waves.
13. Stay within arm's reach of any child.
14. If it starts to rain, get out of the water. It is dangerous to swim during lightning and thunderstorms.
15. Avoid swimming in the ocean for a few days after a big storm. If you do get in the water, wear goggles and earplugs to protect your eyes and ears from infection.
16. Wear a flotation device or a life jacket if you are not a strong swimmer.

HAZARDS AND DANGERS

Bluebottles

In summer, bluebottles are common. You will sometimes see them along the shoreline, which is a sign to avoid the water. But sometimes bluebottles wash in suddenly on the tide while you're in the water. If you get stung by a bluebottle, get out the water and put hot water on the sting. The sting will be painful for a few days but will settle down and eventually disappear. You may need to see a doctor or pharmacist.

Dangerous Swells and Shore breaks

Always check the conditions before you enter the water. Speak to the lifeguards if you are uncertain. If you are not a confident swimmer, it's better to avoid the ocean when there are big swells and dangerous shore breaks.

Sandbanks

Never dive headfirst into the water, as there can be shallow sandbanks just below the surface. The flow of the water pushes sand around making the seabed uneven. It can be shallow and deep in unexpected places.

Rips

Sometimes we can get caught in a fast-flowing current called a rip, which carries us out to the open sea.

You can sometimes recognise rips from the shore:

- they are darker in colour and have fewer or no waves
- they can also be brown with foam on the surface
- you may see debris flowing out to sea in the rip

If you get caught in a rip:

- stay calm and try not to panic—it's important to keep your head above water and keep breathing calmly;
- turn around and float on your back—the rip sometimes brings you back to shore as this is often the arc of a rip—it goes out and it comes back in;
- raise your arm to signal you are in distress and call out to other swimmers for help;
- wait for the lifeguards to rescue you;
- do not try to swim towards the shore because you will be swimming against the force of the rip. This will exhaust you. If you are not too tired, try swimming parallel to the shore or towards breaking waves which will help carry you to shore.

IN SUMMARY

- Come with respect and humility.
- Always err on the side of caution.
- Listen to the water—be aware of your environment.
- Keep breathing. Don't Panic. Always stay calm.

www.ingramcontent.com/pod-product-compliance
Ingram Content Group UK Ltd.
Pitfield, Milton Keynes, MK11 3LW, UK
UKHW041952230426
12048UKWH00008B/299